THE LINCOLN POEMS

Dan Guillory

Mayhaven Publishing, Inc

P O Box 557

Mahomet, IL 61853

USA

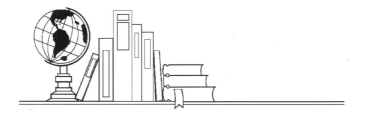

Cover Design: Copyright © 2008 Aaron Porter

Copyright © 2008 Dan Guillory

Library of Congress Control Number: 2007943784

First Edition—First Printing 2008

ISBN 13: 978193227853-8

ISBN 10: 193227853-2

DEDICATION

This book is dedicated to my muses, Leslie and Gayle, and to the Feline Trio of Cleo, Bijou, and Loki who left their prints on the manuscript pages.

Alexander Hay Ritchie's engraved version of Francis Bicknell Carpenter's *The First Reading of the Emancipation Proclamation* (1864). See pages 130-131.

Courtesy of Abraham Lincoln Presidential Library and Museum.

ACKNOWLEDGEMENTS

I happily acknowledge a major debt of gratitude to the Illinois Historic Preservation Agency, and to the following individuals who work in the Abraham Lincoln Presidential Library, in particular Thomas Schwartz (State Historian), Bryon Andreasen (Research Historian), Kathryn Harris (Library Director), Gwen Podeschi (Research Librarian), and Jennifer Ericson (Lincoln Collection).

I am indebted to Jennie Battles (Site Manager - the Vachel Lindsay Home) who graciously sponsored some of the first readings of these poems.

William Furry invited me to work with the Illinois State Historical Society's collection of Block Documents, including the Currier and Ives political cartoons issued during the 1860 presidential campaign. Subsequent presentations on these cartoons made to the McLean County Historical Society in Bloomington and to the Oak Park Historical Society helped shape many of the poems dealing with that period in Lincoln's life.

Bev Hackney, Reference Librarian at the Decatur Public Library, cheerfully helped in ordering books and in sharing resources housed in the Shilling Local History Room.

Brent Wielt of the Macon County Conservation District sponsored a reading of some of the later poems in the book. He was always available to discuss the manuscript in a generous and collegial manner, and he was most helpful in providing materials on the Winter of the Deep Snow (1830).

Curtis Mann, Keith Housewright, and Malinda Garvert of the Sangamon Valley Collection at the Lincoln Library in Springfield helped in many ways, large and small, over the years, especially with books on Vandalia and Lincoln's early years.

A special note of thanks goes to Roland Klose, editor of the Springfield *Illinois Times*, who kindly published several of these poems in the "Lincoln birthday" issues of the newspaper in the years 2004, 2005, 2006, and 2007.

Finally, an extra special note of thanks to Leslie Guillory (my wife) and Gayle Guillory (my daughter), who always matched my excitement over the progress of the book. They made me feel as if it all really mattered—and that I was truly loved.

—DLG
Findlay, Illinois
October 2007

PREFACE
Lincoln and Poetry

Lincoln loved poetry. For most of his adult life he regaled his friends and companions with impromptu recitations of his two favorite poems, rather doleful verses which he quoted in their entirety: Oliver Wendell Holmes' "The Last Leaf" and a poem by the lesser-known Scottish Presbyterian, William Knox, which was entitled "Mortality." It contained the following stanza, which Lincoln admired profoundly:

Oh! Why should the spirit of mortal be proud?
Like a swift-fleeting meteor, a fast-flying cloud,
A flash of lightning, a break of the wave,
He passeth from life to his rest in the grave.

Such morbid and fatalistic sentiments were part of the common emotional vocabulary of the day. Nineteenth-century American culture was obsessed by death and the afterlife. An elegiac mood seemed to pervade the entire country. Huge park-like cemeteries were constructed everywhere, as in the notable example of Gettysburg, where Lincoln delivered his most poetic address on November 19, 1863.

Yet Lincoln also liked lighter fare. He took genuine pleasure in his delivery of Robert Burns' "Tam o'Shanter: A Tale." He always delighted in Shakespeare, especially the tragedies of *Macbeth*, *Hamlet*, and *Richard III*. He was particularly fond of Claudius' soliloquy in *Hamlet*, which begins, "O, my offense is rank. . . ." Lincoln wrote doggerel in the few copybooks and schoolbooks he was able to hoard as the family moved around from southern Indiana to Macon County, Illinois. In 1844, the self-assured young lawyer returned to his old home near Little Pigeon Creek in Indiana, in much the same way that English poet William Wordsworth made his famous pilgrimage to Tintern Abbey. Overcome by nostalgia, Lincoln composed the lyrical poem "My Childhood Home," and the lively narrative "The Bear Hunt," as well as a moving portrait of Matthew, a psychologically disturbed friend from his childhood. About two decades later, Commander in Chief Lincoln often sent messages to Union generals in the form of pithy, rhymed verses.

If he had survived the decade of the 1860's, Lincoln would certainly have written his presidential memoirs—and he may well have turned to the genre of poetry, a medium which would have allowed him to give vent to the emotions he so carefully concealed and controlled for the duration of his adult life. The one event that shattered his emotional insulation was the death of Willie, his favorite son, who died in the White House on February 20, 1862.

The burden of this book is to supply poetry in the putative voice of Lincoln himself, touching on a wide range of subjects, including historically verifiable events as well as imagined experiences that have a high degree of plausibility. For most of his life, Lincoln inhabited the vast Illinois prairie. He had powerful, firsthand encounters with the vagaries of Illinois weather, the painterly beauty of the prairie in springtime, and the characteristically long and luminous sunsets. These poems, however, are not intended to chart or identify epiphanies or "peak moments" in Lincoln's life. The goal, rather, is to dramatize small, transcendent moments when the all-too-rational Lincoln was carried beyond himself, even if only for an instant. We know the precise day Lincoln had a tooth pulled, the particular day he gave a speech in his socks, and the exact day he wrote a $5.00 check to a one-legged man he encountered on the streets of Washington, not far from the White House. Yet we don't have helpful documentation for the encyclopedia of feelings he must have entertained for his wife, sons, legal work, political life, and the frontier environment generally. Hence, this book of poems.

Format and Design

Lincoln was an autodidact who taught himself grammar, rhetoric, law, trigonometry, geometry, and astronomy, among other things. He accumulated a great deal of folklore and on-the-job wisdom as a lawyer for the Eighth Judicial Circuit Court, but he never sloughed off his rural Kentucky twang. For all his life, Lincoln pronounced *chair* as if it were *cheer.* In his dialectal speech, *education* became *eddication.* Even his own English surname became *Linkhorn* or *Linkern.* Lincoln's written English was another matter entirely. He carefully drafted his speeches, aided no doubt by the lawyerly habit of preparing summations and openings for trial juries—and by his lifelong reading of the *King James Bible.* Lincoln wrote excellent English; thus this book does not attempt to reproduce his Kentucky spoken "yawp," but every effort is made to respect Lincoln's favorite rhetorical devices, especially antitheses, and his thoroughly nineteenth-century habit of capitalizing key words to achieve emphasis. Lincoln's love of commas, which caused him considerable trouble with the Superintendent of the Government Printing Office, Mr. John Defrees, is also given free reign in these pages. In his humorous story-telling and droll anecdotes, Lincoln often employed expletives and the occasional vulgarism, but these salty forms of English do not appear in his formal writings. Lincoln always commanded a wide range of diction, from ironic, humorous, and clever badinage to meditative, spiritual, and lofty utterance. He was a master of the language.

These poems began as a sonnet series devoted to the romantic relationship of Anne Rutledge and the young Lincoln of New Salem Village. That project was fueled by the scholarship of John Simon and John Walsh in particular. The original project was abandoned because the sonnet proved to be an unmanageable vehicle for some of the longer poems in this volume. The sonnet heritage persists, however, in the structure and length of many of the shorter poems, which hover around the fourteen-line limit of the traditional form. In like manner, traditional rhyming was de-emphasized while a less intrusive texture of near- and slant-rhyming was inscribed in nearly every poem.

The poems were "field-tested" before audiences at such venues as the Society for the Study of Midwestern Literature at Michigan State University (East Lansing), the Decatur (Illinois) Public Library, and the Vachel Lindsay Home (Springfield, Illinois). The methodology and organization of the poems became the subject of presentations at the annual conferences of the Illinois State Historic Society (2005) and the Illinois Historic Preservation Agency (2006). It quickly became obvious that even well-read audiences found some kind of historical context helpful as an entrée to the poems themselves. The printed texts of each poem were thus preceded by a cultural and historical introduction, in the manner of the Japanese *haibun,* which combines prose and poetry. This format also recalls the "glosses" and marginalia of English writers like Samuel Taylor Coleridge, particularly in "Kubla Khan" and *The Rime of the Ancient Mariner.* Several aesthetic advantages accrued from this arrangement, and the poems actually became sharper in the process.

Naturally, a great deal of scholarly reading and research informs the headnotes to the poems, and the author was fortunate to have world-class resources conveniently available in the form of the Sangamon Valley Collection of the Lincoln Library and the newly-constructed Abraham Lincoln Presidential Library and Museum, both in nearby Springfield. Additional materials were located at the Shilling Local History Room of the Decatur Public Library. It is impossible to list all of the books that helped to engender these poems, but from the deep background of literary consciousness, three titles deserve special mention: Eliza Farnham, *Life in Prairie Land* (1846), Edgar Lee Masters, *Spoon River Anthology* (1915), and John Knoepfle, *Poems from the Sangamon* (1985). The following novels also catalyzed my imagination: Gore Vidal, *Lincoln,* and Richard Slotkin, *Abe.*

The major scholarly books on Lincoln literally fill one library, and the ancillary titles—memoirs, letters, and journals from his contemporaries—would easily fill another. Many of these titles are credited in the prefatory notes to specific poems, but there would have been no book of Lincoln poems without the special insight of Benjamin Thomas, Richard Current, David Donald, Michael Burlingame, Ronald White, Allen Guelzo, Douglas Wilson, Garry Wills, Daniel Epstein, Doris Kearns Goodwin, and Richard Carwardine. Any mistakes in interpretation are obviously mine, not theirs.

TABLE OF CONTENTS

Seeds   16

Winter of the Deep Snow, 1830-1831   18

Picturing the Prairie: New Salem, 1832   20

Ergo Sum   22

Keeping Store With Berry, 1833   24

New Salem Village, 1834   26

Surveying, August 1834   28

Hummingbirds, for Annie   30

Deism in Little Things   32

Vandalia, December 1835   34

Readings   36

Sleeping with Speed, 1837   38

Springfield   40

Lyceum, January 1838   42

Old Buck, 1841   44

Pulling Teeth in Tremont   46

"Love is Eternal"—November 4, 1842   48

Living on the Globe, Nov. 4, 1842   50

Litany for Mary T.   52

Pigs in Taylorville   56

Inventing Jazz   58

Backporch, Eighth and Jackson, August 1846   60

Jane's Piano, December 1849   62

Euclid   64

Geese in Shelby County, November 1851   66

Mud Hole, 1850   68

Milking, 1854   70

Whiggery   72

Blackberrying with Willie, Summer 1855   74

Wintering   76

Eating Illinois   78

The Lost Speech, May 29, 1856   80

Choke Cherries, 1856   82

The Almanac Trial   84

Notes on the August Heat   88

Socks in Danville, September 21, 1858   90

Auf Deutsch, Bitte!   92

Ice Cream at the Smiths   94

Sitting for Brady, February 27, 1860   96

Edward A. Barnwell, Photographer   98

Asleep in Decatur, May 10, 1860   100

Butler's Ambrotype, August 13, 1860   102

On Growing a Beard   104

Billy the Barber, February 10, 1861   106

Cutting and Pasting   108

Willie and Tad, September 1861   110

Flub Dubs   112

The Bottom is Out of the Tub   114

Reading *Hamlet*   116

Constipation   118

Jip   120

Tom Thumb at the White House, February 13, 1863   122

The One Legged Man, August 11, 1863   124

Plug   126

Keckly, Dressing My Hair   128

Carpenter's Allegory   130

Oysters at Willard's   132

City Point, 1865   134

Contents of my Pockets, April 14, 1865   136

Bullet in My Brain, April 15, 1865   138

Alternate Ending   140

SEEDS

Oxford historian Richard Carwardine tells the following story about the future sixteenth president. As a very young lad living with his mother, father, and sister on a hardscrabble farm in Knob Creek, Kentucky, Abraham Lincoln learned an invaluable lesson about the transient and ephemeral nature of all human enterprises. One day he worked slavishly to clear a small patch of ground on which he planted pumpkins. Suddenly a torrential spring downpour washed away every trace of his work and diligence. Lincoln's family would soon make the trip across the Ohio River and settle in Spencer (now Perry) County Indiana, near Little Pigeon Creek. It was there that young Abraham learned to write, often casting his thoughts in the form of short, pithy verses.

Seeds in ground—

Thundersound.

Seeds washed away

By the end of the day.

WINTER of the DEEP SNOW, 1830-1831

Thomas Lincoln and his extended family arrived in Decatur, Illinois in mid-March 1830, spending the night in their wagon and on the open ground between the few cabins standing at that time. The place is now known as Lincoln Square. Guided by their relative, John Hanks, the Lincoln family settled on a high bluff overlooking the Sangamon River, about ten miles west of Decatur in what is now Harristown Township. They quickly cleared the ground, relying on Abraham's considerable skill as a woodsman. They erected a simple cabin, and Abraham made several trips from there to Decatur to purchase "Peruvian bark," the home remedy for malarial infections afflicting various family members. Abraham also gave his first political speech that summer, in front of Harrell's Store, advocating improved navigation of the Sangamon. That winter a meteorologically significant event occurred, the so-called Winter of the Deep Snow, when snow and ice were deposited layer after layer, upon the surface of the prairie until a mass four feet thick covered the entire area. The temperature stayed below freezing in the daytime, dipping to thirty or forty below zero at night. The Lincoln cabin, like most other dwellings at the time, was poorly insulated, with just a single chimney to provide a modicum of heat. Lincoln himself slept in a crude loft only a few feet under the snow-covered roof. Residents of Macon County who died during this terrible ordeal could not be buried because of the frozen ground. Barns and sheds were turned into makeshift morgues. Wild animals and cattle perished as they became stuck in the thick crust of ice. Survivors of this winter of 1830 proudly called themselves "Snowbirds," and they became charter members of the Old Settlers of Macon County. The Lincoln family abandoned this first home site after the spring thaws of 1831, Abraham ultimately settling in New Salem and Thomas setting up house at Goose Nest Prairie near Charleston. In *Early American Winters, Vol. 2: 1821-1870*, David M. Ludlum states that the central Illinois winters were especially harsh from 1830 until 1845, unlike the decade of the 1820's, when the snow was only "shin deep."

Wind slashes through the chinks,

Saber-strokes scoring my ribs, foils

Of ice puncturing my lungs.

My breath turns blue, ice-

Crystals collect on the cabin walls

And the dirt floor hardens into stone.

We are eating parched grains of corn,

Huddled like animals around

The sad embers of a dying hearth.

No food, no firewood, keeping

Our grotesque vigil, moribund

In a zero world become a morgue.

PICTURING the PRAIRIE: NEW SALEM, 1832

Lincoln took up residence in New Salem in July 1831, and shortly thereafter he began working in Denton Offut's store. In 1832, he participated in the Black Hawk War, affording him a larger acquaintance with the Illinois prairie. Although crude forms of photography were being attempted at this time, it was not until 1839 that the French painter and inventor, Louis J. M. Daguerre perfected the *daguerreotype*, which was the first commercially viable form of photography. Thus, the earliest portrait and landscape photographs date to about 1840. Lincoln had a lifelong fascination with technology and new inventions. In fact, in 1858, he delivered a lecture on "Discoveries and Inventions" in several Illinois cities, including Bloomington, Jacksonville, Decatur, Springfield, and Pontiac. Lincoln also applied for a naval patent for one of his ideas, and he showed a keen interest in military technology during the Civil War, enjoying the test-firing of new weaponry. The vast panorama of the Illinois prairie presented Lincoln with an entirely new landform, utterly different from the wooded hills and ravines of southern Indiana.

I insert myself into the corner of a photograph

Black-bordered (it is the Prairie)—

Some years before Daguerre, Parisian inventor

Of photography. I imagine the oversized box camera,

The iris stopped down to admit the bubbling

Half-light of October, these sunflowers

Squeezed into focus, bachelor buttons, tufts

Of pussy willows, sumac, and the lavender parachutes

Of thistles, that's where I set the wobbly tripod

And wait for the warmish breeze to soften and deflate

So Queen Anne's lace, goldenrod, and ragweed

Stiffen into picture-perfect impressions

On a chemically-treated metallic plate.

Yes, I love Science but value Memory

More—every line of Kirkham's *Grammar*

I have by heart, I have the crenellations

Of every leaf and weed, how sure

I am of myself, if only these plants

And undulating hardpan sod, well-rooted

In bluestem, could take measure of my

Greatness, Longshanks would be famous

For the heavy hour required to gel

This photograph, which will be invented

Shortly and Time itself will ooze chemically

While I walk through the corn shocks,

Stepping out of the frame into the other Reality.

ERGO SUM

Mr. Kim Bauer, formerly Curator of the Henry Horner Collection of Lincoln artifacts at the Illinois Historic Preservation Agency, and now head of Lincoln tourism in Decatur, believes that Lincoln, above all else, was a narcissist. And Lincoln did burn the proverbial midnight oil, especially during his New Salem days. Descartes' famous dictum, "I think therefore I am," may be read as the beginning of all self-referential modern thought.

Cogito ergo sum.—Descartes

Silence keeps busy talking to itself

As if that will bring on the Night:

Where even the blue crickets and garrulous

Gnats have closed the big shop

And nothing moves, not even an arrow

Of dust, falling on the faceless Prairie.

Now is the best of times to tell the truth—

Running a finger on the store-bought blade,

Pushing the point into the whorl of the thumb

So a little planet of blood oozes

And spins into a jellied globe, congealing

Under that snowball of Lunar Light

Or the sad tallowed flame of old Cogitation.

KEEPING STORE with BERRY, 1833

On January 15, 1833, while in residence at New Salem, Lincoln and William F. Berry purchased a general store from William Greene for $750, although they had previously held joint ownership in a smaller store at the end of 1832. Berry obtained a liquor license for the new store in his own name, a point Lincoln made again and again as Stephen Douglas tried to accuse him of being a tavern-keeper. Berry had no head for business, and he apparently stayed tipsy on the whisky he was trying to sell. In any event, the store failed utterly or, in Lincoln's words, "winked out." Lincoln also served as postmaster for New Salem during this period, and, after he was elected to the Illinois State Legislature in 1834, he and his fellow Whigs joined with the Democrats and led the fight to create an "Illinois System" of roads, canals, and railroads, borrowing some ten million dollars. The whole scheme collapsed during the Panic of 1837, plunging the state into near bankruptcy. It took the state forty years to pay off its debts, with only a canal to show for the efforts. Lincoln also spent several years paying off his own personal debt incurred because of the failure of the Lincoln-Berry store. He whimsically referred to it as "the national debt."

Think of the State of Illinois as a giant store,

With citizens as customers, perpetually eager

To buy licenses, offices, certificates, and deeds.

The store borrows ten million dollars for inventory

When suddenly the banks run out of money,

And the Great State of Illinois closes its doors,

Turning its customers away, much like Lincoln

And Berry, store-keepers of musty cheese and calico

So ugly that absolutely no one would buy it.

Entrepreneurship is a calling and a kind of religion.

And I was faithful, a zealot to the very end—

Even if my fickle god kept looking the other way.

NEW SALEM VILLAGE, 1834

Lincoln lived in New Salem from July 1831 to April 14, 1837. Here he became a student, borrowing books from farmers and from the ill-prepared schoolmaster, Mentor Graham. Here he learned to appreciate the poetry of Robert Burns and Shakespeare under the boozy tutelage of Jack Kelso, who took Lincoln on as his fishing partner. Jack Armstrong challenged the young but strong Lincoln to a wrestling match and lost, thereafter becoming a lifelong friend and supporter. New Salem and its residents, especially young Abraham Lincoln, were all discovering the pleasures of potentiality.

Smoke licks the clouds, and every cedared roof

Finds its pointed place in the blueness

Of October, river birch and shagbark hickory

Dropping color-coded messages everywhere.

Old Jack Kelso is sober this morning: he savors

The first frost as Jack Kelso eats side meat and hominy.

Mentor Graham, hair a-flutter, lugs the new-bound

Leather books he can hardly teach—

But we all reach, trying to be better

Or even just as good

As everything so abundantly *here:*

Coneflowers ringed in frost,

The mirrored panels of daylight

Letting me step out of my Old Life

And into the New.

SURVEYING, AUGUST 1834

With only the equivalent of a third-grade education, Lincoln the auto-
didact taught himself trigonometry in order to become a surveyor, a
profession he practiced successfully from 1834 to 1836, while official-
ly residing in New Salem and spending part of the year in Vandalia. He
probably relied on Robert Gibson's *A Treatise on Practical Surveying*
(1803), one of the basic handbooks of the day. Lincoln platted the near-
by town of Petersburg, up the Sangamon River from New Salem, as
well as the village of New Boston in Mercer County.

My sweet-ribbed prairie is breaking its back

In this August heat, bellowed into tunnels of air,

Cracked open into tents of light, apertures

And spaces neatly receiving

Carpentered cedar-shakes, ridgepoles,

Corn cribs and thc waggling Bluestem,

Everything given a proper place in the Ether.

I sit in the shadows, searching for pain

While I dream of dreaming—*sine* this,

Cosine that—my long hard heart is pinched

Into place. I have plotted every inch:

The seen / the unseen. Compass, rod,

And chain, a boundary line of birds

Stretching link by link over the splintered

Creek while the same sun cools down, slower

And slower in the earthen kiln of the Prairie.

HUMMINGBIRDS for ANNIE

Recent scholarship by Professors John Simon and John Walsh has shown that the amorous relationship between Abraham Lincoln and Anne Rutledge was, indeed, a factual occurrence, as argued many years ago by Billy Herndon, Lincoln's law partner, shortly after the President's death. Mary and Robert Lincoln vociferously objected to any mention of Anne. Yet Lincoln did give Anne his precious copy of Kirkham's *Grammar*, inscribed with the words, "Ann M. Rutledge is now learning Grammar." She died tragically on August 25, 1835.

Paired hummingbirds

Hanging in the air

Golden-green

Iridescent as beetles . . .

High in the sycamores

Cicadas scrape out

The last true song of Summer—

Tones of grass and crook-necked

Gourds, the sweet cider of Memory:

Dream-girl, Flower-girl

Annie in the Mayapples

Annie picking Trout-Lilies

Annie with her nose to a Coneflower.

Her hair smelled like rain.

She wore her skin

Like a store-bought suit of clothes.

Now, under a wet, fermenting moon

I pick my violet Bachelor Buttons

Placing them dreamwise

In the little button-hole of Love.

DEISIM in LITTLE THINGS

During his New Salem days Lincoln wrote an article on "Infidelity," which one of his friends promptly burned lest it get the young iconoclastic author into trouble. Lincoln was enamored of deism and enlightenment philosophy in general. In fact, at no time in his life did Lincoln profess a belief in the divinity of Jesus Christ (a view also held by Ralph Waldo Emerson) or in the validity of the trinity. But he continued to read and study sacred scripture. At some point in this early period of his life, Lincoln read a treatise that was popular with the intellectuals of the day—*Volney's Ruins; or Meditation on the Revolutions of Empires*, written by Constantin Francois Volney and originally published in Paris. Lincoln undoubtedly read an English translation, probably the New York edition, published by Dickson and Sickels in 1828. Volney appended a special chapter to the work entitled "The Law of Nature," which listed ten attributes of Nature: it is "Primitive, Immediate, Universal, Invariable, Evident, Reasonable, Just, Pacific, Beneficent, and Alone Sufficient." These qualities may have seemed to inhere in Anne Rutledge, who not only was Lincoln's sweetheart but also his fellow student. They had even planned to attend college together in Jacksonville before her tragic demise on August 25, 1835, on the Rutledge family farm, some seven miles northwest of New Salem. Purkapile Creek flowed near the Rutledge farm and was well known to the villagers of New Salem. For a few weeks, at least, Lincoln was shattered by Anne's death. He reported that he could not bear the thought of rain or snow falling on her grave. Anne is also the subject of one of the most famous poems in Masters' *Spoon River Anthology.* She is now buried in the cemetery in nearby Petersburg.

The ice on Purkapile Creek is flattened

Into a little crystal floor, and the curve

Of Annie's breast makes a perfect

Parabola of Immediate Beauty,

Redeeming the very soul of my Soul.

Her hands—the cathedral where I come

To worship, her lips the portal to everything

That is Universal and Sufficient.

VANDALIA, DECEMBER 1835

Before Springfield, Vandalia served as the state capital of Illinois—and as political nurse of Abraham Lincoln. He served as a state legislator from Jan. 6, 1834, until the state capital was moved to Springfield on December 9, 1839, largely at the instigation of Lincoln and the famous "Long Nine" legislators of Sangamon County. Vandalia was truly a rough-and-tumble venue, like most Illinois towns of the 1830's, but Lincoln learned firsthand the seamy and celestial sides of state politics. When he was in town, Lincoln usually lodged at the Charter Hotel, a rough, two-story wooden building across from the Capitol building. At this point in time, Lincoln was still the cocky young man, trying very hard to make his mark in the world.

Sluices of mud, green gashes

Of hogshit and hard boiled shirtings

Frozen on the line. The empty sleeves

Wave as I make my way upon the ice.

This town needs a decent house

Of Indecency, a snake-oil merchant

And a bookseller with Eastern books to hand.

City fathers pay a wolf bounty here—

Fifty cents for a small pelt

Dollar for a large—

That buys you four nights in a cheap hotel.

Now I sympathize with the Illinois Wolf

Giving up his hide

So some scoundrel can get a good night's sleep.

READINGS

As an autodidact, Lincoln read voraciously even in his early years in Spencer County, Indiana where books were hard to come by. He continued his self-education in New Salem, and later in Springfield, especially after making Billy Herndon his law partner. Herndon regularly brought books to their office for Lincoln to peruse. Lincoln's reading list included the Bible, the poetry of Robert Burns, Shakespeare (especially *Richard III, Macbeth,* and *Hamlet*), and Blackstone's *Commentaries on English Law.* He also studied Bingham's *Columbian Orator* (1816), Kirkham's *Grammar* (1818), and the enlightenment philosophy of Volney's *Ruins* (1828). In later life, Lincoln studied Euclid rigorously to compensate for his lack of formal education. Lincoln had strong streaks of narcissism and solipsism in his make-up, so he found deep, meditative readings practically irresistible.

At first, I read books—

Shakespeare, Volney, Burns

And Blackstone, the columns

Of text planted like Illinois corn.

But the Prairie was my true Grammarian,

The small, bright Orations of springtime,

The unforgiving syntax of Winter, each flake

A cognate of its fellows.

It is a Library, all this turning

Of leaves, growing older day

By day, reading the Lexicons

As if to find that ineffable Word.

SLEEPING with SPEED, 1837

In his recent book, *The Intimate World of Abraham Lincoln*, C. A. Tripp argues that Lincoln was a homosexual, partly because he shared his bed with other men. This practice was inevitable in the pioneer days of Illinois, largely because there were not enough beds to go around, so travelers and boarders were forced to sleep together. Lincoln arrived in Springfield on April 15, 1837, and promptly arranged lodgings with Joshua Speed, who ran a store at Fifth and Washington. Lincoln was penniless at the time, but they quickly became intimate friends. After Speed returned to his native Louisville in January, 1841, the two men stayed in touch, as this period marked the break-up of Mary and Abraham, and Lincoln sorely required a confidant. He spent three weeks with Speed in Louisville from late August to early September in 1841. Joshua Speed was perhaps the only real friend of Abraham Lincoln, a man who was inscrutable and aloof for all of his life.

Above the pickle barrels, the crocks of salted pork,

The bolts of calico cloth, the shovels, scythes,

And agricultural tools, we make our humble bed.

The usual things—women, money, the weather,

The existence of a just God, slavery, marriage—

A lot of hot air and occasional gas.

This is friendship, sharing a too-small cover,

Giving up your painful secrets, waiting in sleep

For reassurance as pure as morning light.

SPRINGFIELD

On a visit to the "Sucker State," as Illinois was nicknamed (after a small fish found in Illinois streams), the writer Washington Irving remarked, "Illinois is full of children and dogs." He might well have added hogs to the list because they were a common sight on the main streets and alleys of most Illinois towns. Paul Angle has given us an excellent portrait of Springfield in Lincoln's day in his classic book, *"Here I Have Lived": A History of Lincoln's Springfield, 1821-1865* (1935). Of course, Springfield would not have become the state capital in 1837 had it not been for the "wire-pulling" of Lincoln and the famous "Long Nine" legislators of Sangamon County. Most commentators on nineteenth-century Springfield note the prevalence of hogs in the streets. Like it or not, they became the unofficial mascots of the place. On wet days, their filth mingled with the mud and slush. On dry, windy days, their leavings became part of the dust inhaled by the entire population. The porkers were, like the bureaucrats and legislators, the most visible ambassadors of the city. An eyewitness description of the Springfield street scene at this time occurs in John Hancock's sonnets. Writing under the pen name "H," Hancock was an observant Englishman who tended bar in Springfield before moving back to England. In 1982, Illinois literary historian John Hallwas edited *The Poems of H., the Lost Poet of Lincoln's Springfield.*

On searingly hot days, their dung

Dries into dusty flakes, inhaled

By the fair citizenry of Springfield,

Already burdened by the acrid smell

Of lobbyists and legislators—and

With the horses, they render the air un-

Breathable. Perhaps we should pass

Entirely new laws against the passing

Of all future laws, or license those hogs

With the decency to conceal their doings.

LYCEUM, JANUARY 1838

Elijah Lovejoy was a radical Presbyterian minister from New England who simultaneously espoused powerful abolitionist and anti-Catholic views. "Popery" was one of his most frequently uttered words. Reverend Lovejoy settled in Saint Louis where the indignant pro-Southern and largely Catholic population drove him and his newspaper, the *Observer*, across the Mississippi to Alton, Illinois. Once in Alton, Lovejoy continued his highly inflammatory campaign. Irate mobs destroyed two of his printing presses by dumping them into the Mississippi River. Finally, in November 1837, a third mob burned down the warehouse where a third printing press was housed—and they shot Lovejoy dead. He instantly became a martyr for the national abolitionist cause. Lincoln, as David Donald has ably shown, exhibited a complex reaction to this troubling turn of events. On the one hand, he abhorred mob violence and the quashing of religious expression and freedom of the press. On the other hand, he loathed the virulent anti-Catholic rhetoric, which was the trademark of this firebrand minister cum editor. Lincoln had become greatly concerned about the deleterious effects of mob action and rabble-rousing in general, which he feared would undermine and ultimately destroy a rational, constitutionally-based society. These thoughts were clearly in the foreground when, some three months after Lovejoy's death, Lincoln addressed the Young Men's Lyceum of Springfield on the topic of "The Perpetuation of Our Political Institutions." Lincoln exhorted the young men to avoid "wild and furious passions" and to revere the laws as a form of a national "political religion." Owen Lovejoy, Elijah's brother who lived in northern Illinois ultimately became a U.S. congressman and an important ally of the president. Lincoln came to depend heavily on evangelical Christians, especially the Methodists and Presbyterians, who voted as blocs in the elections of 1860 and 1864, although he personally was never affiliated with any denomination.

Loss of control is equally loss

Of the Self—our Reason and Judgment

Are all. We cannot execute editors or

Ministers of god, nor submerge

The leaden characters of Democracy

In the muddy-bottomed Mississippi

While maintaining any vestige of Humanity.

So, Reverend Lovejoy, adieu, and may

The multitude of slaves you died to save

Discover some small measure of Peace

In this most bellicose of republics,

Unsafe, even for white evangelicals.

OLD BUCK, 1841

From 1839 until 1860, Lincoln was a member of the Eighth Judicial Circuit Court, riding with his friend Judge David Davis to such places as Tremont, Mt. Pulaski, Metamora, Bloomington, Urbana, Danville Monticello, Shelbyville, Sullivan, Decatur, and Taylorville. He was thus forced to leave Mary and the boys at home in Springfield for weeks—or even months—at a time. Life on the circuit was hard, but Lincoln forged many relationships as a traveling lawyer and fattened his purse in the process. He went where the work and the people were to be found. Food on the road was sometimes execrable, and private accommodations were virtually unknown. Sleeping three or four to a bed was a common practice since furniture, like money, was hard to find on the frontier. A typical supper might consist of salt pork, beans, and cornpone. Then, after socializing around the hearth, the lawyers would retire to a corn shuck mattress, which they often shared with two or more strangers. Conditions ameliorated considerably by the late 1840's and early 1850's, when proper hotels were built in the larger cities. Old Buck was Lincoln's favorite horse on these expeditions into the Heartland, either saddled or pulling a buggy. Blackstone's *Commentaries on English Law* was the standard legal reference tool of the day.

Old Buck sways in line with the Prairie, as if

Thinking "horizons were made for old gray horses."

He listens all too patiently while I rehearse cases,

A junior partner who always knows his place.

He knows when to canter, when to trot,

And how much of a load his back can bear.

Judge Davis rides ahead, a behemoth in a buggy,

Three hundred pounds of legal corpulence.

Tonight, we'll sup on more fat pork and pone

As Buck savors the local timothy and hay.

Then, a tallow candle, a little Blackstone,

Maybe time to scratch out a letter home.

Bedding down with the Lawyer for the Defense

Who farts all night, carefully punctuating his brief.

PULLING TEETH in TREMONT

On October 20, 1841, a dentist in Tremont, Illinois pulled one of Lincoln's teeth, in the process "bringing with it a bit of the jawbone." Lincoln also complained that he could "neither talk, nor eat." *Quo warranto* is a lawyer's expression meaning "by what authority." In point of fact, Lincoln did not sue the dentist, no matter how painful the experience was. Tremont, Illinois was originally part of the Eighth Judicial Circuit Court, also serving as the county seat of Tazewell County until that distinction was given to Pekin in 1850. Lincoln tried many cases in Tremont, and he was very well known there. Located about fifty miles northeast of Springfield, Tremont was the first stop for all the lawyers following the old Eighth Circuit.

Woe to this petty tyrant of Tremont,

A terrible tooth-extractor, with talents

More suited to veterinarian practice

And teeth of equine or bovine proportions.

Why, I shall sue by writ of *Quo warranto*!

By what authority does he torture un-

Suspecting victims in his hard wooden chair,

Removing the tooth while shattering

The tender and protective jaw!

Now, unable to eat or speak, I seek

Just compensation and punitive damages

For having lost those unappreciated

Faculties that make me singularly human.

"LOVE is ETERNAL"—NOVEMBER 4, 1842

Mary Ann Todd and Abraham Lincoln courted passionately during the latter months of 1840, but Lincoln suddenly broke off the engagement (or mutual understanding) on New Year's day, 1841, plunging himself into a fit of depression or "hypochondria," as he called it, for which he received medical treatment. Much later, through the agency of Simeon Francis, editor of the *Sangamo Journal*, the couple found a safe meeting place, and the relationship was resumed. They were married hastily and with no advance notice—even to Mary's censorious family—on the evening of November 4, 1842, with Reverend Charles Dresser, an Episcopalian minister who later sold them his house at Eighth and Jackson, performing the wedding ceremony. Lincoln had visited Chatterton's Jewelry Store on the west side of the square to buy a wedding ring with the inscription "A. L. to Mary, Nov. 4, 1842: Love is Eternal." Lincoln must have been one of the first customers of jeweler-silversmith George Chatterton because he and his brother Charles had opened the store on October 28, 1842, only a week prior to the Lincoln's wedding. Lincoln's passionate love of books, law books in particular, was well established in New Salem and during his early years in Springfield, after April 15, 1837, when he moved in with Joshua Speed, whose store was close to Chatterton's establishment.

Sweet Mary, I am schoolboy at your side, student

Of the bound volume abundant with information.

The theme, the meaning, develops as a series

Of impressions under my fingertips.

A little crease here, some dog-eared flap—

Gently thumbing the well-tooled spine.

There is reassurance in the familiar—

Sadness at the inevitable ending.

And perfect pleasure, reading it again

As if for the very first time.

LIVING on the GLOBE, Nov. 4, 1842

After an on-again, off-again engagement with Lexington socialite Mary Todd, Lincoln hurriedly married the plump young woman, to the apparent horror of her relatives—the Ninian W. Edwards family, who considered Lincoln a marriage below her station, although the wedding occurred at the Edwards residence. In any event, the hastily arranged ceremony occurred on the evening of November 4, 1842, and the couple skipped their honeymoon and moved directly into the Globe Tavern on Adams Street. The Globe Tavern changed hands many times, and many additions and name changes occurred until it was finally torn down about 1880. According to Ralph Gary in *Following in Lincoln's Footsteps*, the couple's room may have been as small as eight by fourteen feet. A week after they settled in, Lincoln left for work on the Eighth Circuit Court in Christian County, desperate to improve his financial condition. Nearly nine months to the day after their arrival, Abraham and Mary greeted their firstborn, Robert Lincoln, on August 1, 1843. *Drummer* is nineteenth-century slang for traveling salesman; *draymen* drove wagons, carts, or *drays*. "Delicacy" was the euphemism for pregnancy.

Whiskey drummers, itinerant preachers, draymen

And politicians. Manure in the street, tobacco juice

On the floors. And here we honeymoon!

A capital hotel in the capital of wilderness.

Four dollars a week for boiled dinners, salt pork

And potatoes, eight by fourteen square feet in a dry

Box of a room. Sweet joys of matrimony—Mary Ann's

"Delicacy" more visible day by wintering day.

Is this the best the world has to offer, the sum

Of the Globe's riches? She squeezes between

The few sticks of furniture, and I am off

To Christian County, making money, I hope.

LITANY for MARY T.

As Jean Baker points out in her detailed biography, Mary Todd was an aristocratic young woman from Lexington, Kentucky, who was raised with slaves and educated to speak French and talk politics like a man. Her family members were diehard supporters of Henry Clay (as was Lincoln). When she moved to Springfield in 1839 to escape the clutches of her hated stepmother, Mary resided with her sister and brother-in-law, Ninian Wirt Edwards. In the closed circle of Springfield society of the 1840's, Mary Todd became the belle of the ball, courted passionately by all the eligible bachelors, including Stephen A. Douglas and awkward Abraham Lincoln, a fellow Kentuckian. In 1840, however, she and Lincoln became formally engaged, but he broke the engagement on January 1, 1841, under mysterious circumstances. In mid-1842, the couple was brought together by mutual friends, and they began to meet secretly. Suddenly on November 4, 1842, they were married in the Edwards home, Mary's sister complaining of inadequate time to prepare a proper wedding reception. The ceremony was performed by Rev. Charles Dresser, who later sold them his house at Eighth and Jackson. At least two prominent Illinois historians (who chose to cloak themselves in anonymity) believe that Mary actually seduced the diffident young lawyer in order to precipitate the marriage. In any event, their firstborn, Robert Todd, appeared on August 1, 1843—almost exactly nine months later. Throughout her life Mary was famous for her headstrong ways, her impulsive buying habits, and her tempestuous temper. But her life was never easy, with a husband gone circuit-riding for nearly half the year while she struggled to keep house and raise four boys, two of whom were dead before the end of President Lincoln's first term in office. For all the ups and downs of their relationship, Lincoln was deeply and passionately attracted to Mary throughout his life.

O, terrible She
Angel-fat goddess
My tormenting Daemon
In black-toed slippers
My dancing accordion.

She of the seven petticoats
And the slit-open drawers,
Eyes fierce as a lynx
Nakedness all musk and mink.

O, she of the burning gaze
The upcurled lip
The little finger
Hooked behind my ear
That hitching-post of love,

She of the marble knees
The alabaster throat
The breasts of cool pink jade
Nippled in coral.

She of the half-drunk goblet
And the fluted white napkin.
She of the proper fork
And fluent French phrase.

She of the endless purse—
Pillager of millinery shops,
Jewelry and cutlery
Copper silver gold
Brooches pearls pins
Necklaces bracelets gems
Flimsy tulle veils whalebone
Corsets and lacework shawls.

She of the meaty jowls
Eater of roasts and Virginia hams
Candied yams blackberry cobbler
Cool tumblers of buttermilk

Brushing white her hirsute lip.
She of the serpent's tongue
It uncoils with a kiss
Slithers into your mouth
Where the venom
Turns everything into a Lie.
She of the comet-bright hair

With darkly-tufted underarms
The ineffable furrow
Unspeakable furze and fat
Portal of heaven
Gate of Hell.

O, she of the buttery bellyfat
The small tendrils of lust
The pungent crevices
The fermenting dark fruit
Where I am drunken nocturnal fool
Voracious and never satisfied.

PIGS in TAYLORVILLE

During the time he served on the Eighth Judicial Circuit Court, under the watchful eye of his good friend Judge David Davis (whom he later appointed to the Supreme Court), Abraham Lincoln considered Taylorville as his last stop on the circuit before returning home to Springfield. Local tradition has it that, on one occasion, the orderly business of the court was interrupted by a noisy group of porkers under the floor. In a humorous moment, lawyer Lincoln asked Judge Davis for a *Writ of Quietus* against the vociferous hogs and proceeded to coax them away. On May 28, 2005, sculptor John McClarey unveiled his bronze statue, *The Last Stop*, on the Christian County Courthouse lawn, commemorating this event. It is worth speculating whether Lincoln saw the symbolic and metaphorical implications of the pigs, especially after he settled in Washington as the sixteenth president.

Such whining, wheezing, snorting, and grunting—

A guttural affront to the dignity and *gravitas*

Of the court and all legislative proceedings. My

Learned brothers, whether Democrat, Republican,

Or Whig, I say to you, Learn well the lesson

Of big-bellied swine who inhabit the lowest reaches

Of the legal establishment, who wallow tenderly in pools

Of mud, supping on the very scum of the earth, sticking

Their snouts into every unspeakable place—by dint

Of their cacophonous wailings, they shatter the concord

And peacefulness that empower all rational discourse.

Then, utterly exhausted by their efforts, they roll over

On a bed of their own waste, snoring into oblivion.

INVENTING JAZZ

The documented history of Jazz really begins with the Rose Record Company of Chicago and their recording of Louis Armstrong and the Hot Five in 1919. This complex musical form evolved in New Orleans, largely because Union troops abandoned many cornets, drums, horns, and other musical instruments after their Civil War occupation of the city. The early Jazz tunes thus often carry the name of military "marches" like "When the Saints Go Marching In." As the most visible and resonant icon in American civilization, Lincoln is often credited with everything quintessentially American. Although jazz was first performed shortly after Lincoln died, the form is tied to the period of his death—and to the Civil War. Jazz, after all, was the music of the freed slaves. It is also associated with New Orleans and Chicago, places Lincoln certainly knew. *Skiffle* is a kind of "rockabilly" pop music played in England during the 1950's. Professor James Hurt in *Writing Illinois* explains that the first visitors to the landscape of the Illinois Prairie literally had no language with which to describe it. Music can be described as another way of filling space, or another way of telling time. This problem was tackled by French philosopher and phenomenologist Gaston Bachelard in his classic *The Poetics of Space*. Cass County and Beardstown in particular are locally famous for the succulent quality of their melons.

Everything is a metaphor (for something else)

So the Prairie is music (not yet created)—

Not the Ragtime of big city places

But the pure blue notes of tenor saxophone

Hugging the vaulted space, taking down

Boundaries: Christian, Shelby, Sangamon, Menard,

Whole counties reverberating in a slow skiffle

Of snowflakes falling, mulberries rapping

In unstoppable winds. Somewhere

Outside the melon fields of Beardstown

The drummer starts his battered roll,

My spavined horse scatters gravel

And all the Saints go marching in.

BACKPORCH, EIGHTH and JACKSON
AUGUST 1846

The Lincoln family lived at Eighth and Jackson from May 1, 1844 to Feb. 10, 1861. On June 16, 1887 Robert Todd Lincoln gave the Lincoln Home to the State of Illinois, which restored the Home in 1955 and gave it to the National Park Service on Sept. 1, 1971. More restoration work occurred between 1986-1988, and on June 16, 1988, the Home was rededicated. Here Lincoln did a prodigious amount of reading— often to Mary's dismay—and honed his skills as a self-taught rhetorician. In August 1846, while still living in this house, Lincoln defeated Methodist preacher Peter Cartwright, a Democrat, and won a seat in the U. S. Congress. Lincoln had to walk a fine lawyerly line to defend himself against charges of atheism launched by Cartwright during the election. Lincoln managed to make his deist philosophy sound religious while carefully distancing himself from any specific Christian sect.

The sky, suddenly grown verbal,

Murmurs in parables,

Some cloudy constructions,

Certain inflections of indigo and pearl-gray—

An outsider trying to speak the Language,

A syntax of rain and heat,

A bad marriage of grammar and thought.

And, Yes, I know whereof I speak.

JANE'S PIANO, DECEMBER 1849

Jane Martin Johns is one of the most important early residents of Decatur and Macon County, as well as the author of *Personal Recollections*, a fascinating memoir of the period, including anecdotes about Lincoln and many Civil War events. Jane met Lincoln on the very day she arrived in Decatur in December 1849, sorely in need of help to unload her precious piano, which was strapped down in a wagon in front of the Macon House (later the Revere House). Lincoln convinced his lawyer friend from Bloomington, Leonard Swett, to assist, and the two men somehow maneuvered the ungainly instrument into the hotel lobby. Jane rewarded the two young lawyers by treating them to dinner and playing some of the popular tunes of the day afterward, including "Old Dan Tucker."

The law is a marble monument,

Ponderous and immovable.

But Jane's piano is heavier

And makes sweeter music.

Is this the harmony I crave,

The sweet constitution of notes,

The sound of freedom

Unlocked from the keys

Like slaves unshackled

In a land as deaf as ours?

EUCLID

Lincoln was always insecure about his lack of formal education. In his later years, he took up the study of *The Six Books of Euclid*, partly because this form of geometry was the backbone of British public school education at schools like Harrow and Eaton, and partly because it appealed to his sense of logic and to his belief in predestination, the one idea he had adopted from his parents' Baptist congregation in Kentucky. Lincoln loved the inexorable movement from hypothesis to hypothesis and, finally, to a conclusion. Euclid also satisfied his lawyerly cravings for neat chains of causation and logical explanations. Geometry was thus an elegant form of arranging "evidence." Lincoln had earlier studied trigonometry during his New Salem days in order to qualify as a surveyor, and he had always shown an aptitude for mathematics. Without the distraction of modern city glare, Lincoln could easily discern the constellations during clear nights on the vast prairie. He had also picked up a little astronomy during his days of self-study at New Salem, and he would have certainly known the easily recognizable *W*-shape of Cassiopeia, which can be seen above the northeast horizon, between Andromeda and Cepheus.

A line extended, say, from Cassiopeia

To the cowshed behind my home

Will describe a circle as the earth turns.

Another line makes a perfect triangle in-

Visibly supporting the back porch, as moon-

Light is poured through a perfect cone.

It is all a well-made figure, you know—

These motions that we call Living.

There is pattern-making in every Thing:

The uncalculated point where all the lines con-

Verge at the exact place and time of Death.

GEESE in SHELBY COUNTY, NOVEMBER 1851

The Court House in Shelbyville was the natural meeting place for the Eighth Circuit Court sessions, and lawyer Lincoln was there on November 4, 1851, to ply his trade. He probably stayed at the old Tackett House, later the Tallman Hotel. On his way to and from the county seat of Shelby County, he may well have encountered the migratory Canada Goose (*Branta Canadensis*), as Illinois lay athwart the great North American Flyway. These beautiful geese, flying in their distinctive *V*'s, followed this natural avian highway. Today, the Canada Goose has become a year-round resident in all counties of Illinois, unmistakable with its gray body, black head and neck, and distinctive white chin "strap." Lincoln was always a keen observer, with a highly retentive memory. The quill pens, primitive ink, and rough paper of his day provide suitable analogues for this moment.

Squibs of black—

Smudges on snowlight.

Look, I am writing a life

Of sharp-edged details, real

And half-real, like this flight of un-

Countable geese, ascending

Heavenward.

MUD HOLE, 1850

In *Life in Prairie Land* (1846), a vivid and telling memoir of life on the Illinois frontier in the 1830's, Eliza Farnham describes how elegantly dressed ladies from the East met the ghastly reality of springtime in Illinois when their wagons and carriages capsized or sank in the numerous "slews" and mud holes engulfing the primitive roads and trails. Nearly a century would pass before paved roads became common in the farm country that Lincoln knew and loved. The most popular songwriter of the day, Stephen Foster, described a similar problem in his famous tune, "Camptown Races" (1850):

> The long-tailed filly and the big black hoss,
> They plowed up the track and they both run across.
> The black hoss stickin' in a big mud hole—
> They can't touch bottom with a ten-foot pole!

In the antebellum period, ladies' undergarments were designed with slits in the bottom to facilitate their use of outhouses and chamber pots. The women were already seriously encumbered by whalebone corsets, crinolines, and petticoats. Lincoln traveled the old road from New Salem to Springfield many times before settling in Springfield on April 15, 1837.

The roads in Spring Time, like illogical

Arguments, lead to draws, slews,

And bottomless holes. Those sweet ladies

In the overturned buggy, their legs

Flaccid and fish-belly white, open

Their slitted drawers to the sky.

I am on my way to Springfield,

Taking all this as a sign—the Art

Of Politics is apprehending the unmentionable

And pretending that it never happened.

MILKING, 1854

Garry Wills, Ronald White, Daniel Epstein, and Douglas Wilson have all written excellent analyses of Lincoln's style of writing and thinking. Essentially, Lincoln's mind worked somewhat like a computer with its binary "on-off" logic. He tended to see things in terms of paired opposites, and he naturally favored the rhetorical device of antithesis. In his famous "House Divided" speech of 1858, he remarked, in typical fashion, that the "government cannot endure, permanently half *slave* and half *free*." The italics are Lincoln's—he often italicized key words, especially when he wanted to emphasize a contrast. In 1854, Lincoln's perennial opponent, Senator Stephen A. Douglas, engineered the passage of the Kansas Nebraska Act, which allowed for "popular sovereignty" in those vast territories, thus allowing slavery to be introduced in formerly free territory. Lincoln was outraged, and he promptly awoke from his political slumber, becoming one of the most vocal opponents of the bill. The Kansas Nebraska Act became Lincoln's entrée to the national political scene. In the 1840's and 1850's, many Springfield residents still had barns and enough land to maintain a milking cow, as the Lincolns did at their home on the corner of Eighth and Jackson.

In the Springfield morning, smoked with hickory and ash,

I sit on the stool, milking an old dun cow, enjoying

The tinny sound of milk under pressure, as it pings

And drills into my deep wooden bucket.

The udder grows alternately hard, then soft

As I squeeze and finesse, thinking Kansas

Nebraska, North South, Free and Slave.

It must all become one thing—or another.

The teat goes dry in my hand, the bag emptied

At last, warm milk brimming in the bucket,

A dog barking in the distance,

As now the day begins.

WHIGGERY

Under the capable leadership of Henry Clay, the Whig Party of the 1830's evolved as a response to the Democratic policies of Thomas Jefferson and Andrew Jackson. As their name would imply, the Whigs were the party of "loyal opposition," favoring a strong central bank, easing of lines of credit, protective tariffs, and a vast system of internal improvement of canals, waterways, turnpikes, and railroads known as the "American System." The Whigs were basically the party of businessmen—there were no large corporations at the time. Lincoln believed the Whigs would offer opportunities for farmers and factory workers to improve their lot and earn more and more money, ultimately hiring workers of their own. Although Lincoln and the other Illinois Whigs nearly caused the state to go bankrupt in 1837 in their attempt to build a railroad, the goal was sound, even if the financial backing was only on paper. Yet a dozen or so years later, the railroads drastically changed day-to-day life in Illinois. The Whigs were generally opposed to slavery, primarily on economic and constitutional—rather than moral—grounds, but the passage of the Kansas-Nebraska Act in 1854 caused the Whig Party to self-destruct, as many Whigs joined the racist Know-Nothing Party, the Democratic Party led by Stephen Douglas, or the newly-formed Republican Party. The Morrill Land Grant Act of 1862, which Lincoln signed into law, thus creating a new tier of agricultural and mechanical colleges, was essentially the fulfillment of a Whiggish dream. The issuance of paper money during the Civil War and the strong national banking system of Salmon P. Chase were also driven by a Whiggish philosophy. Lincoln personally abhorred manual labor, probably because his father Thomas hired him out to neighbors to take advantage of young Lincoln's rail-splitting skills. Abraham saved his greatest contempt for the occupation of farming, which he regarded as the lowest form of drudgery. He particularly despised his father's subsistence farming which left no margin for profit or prospects for the future. And although Thomas was a fair carpenter and cabinet maker, he made little or no effort to sell his furniture. He could not see beyond the next season.

Consider Thomas Lincoln, farmer,

A man who never grew more corn

Than he could eat, never bought land

When it was cheap—eventually

Borrowing money from his own son

Whom he once rented out like a slave.

He hated books, except for the Bible,

Never staying in one place long enough

To accumulate any wealth. Poverty

Is the ultimate form of slavery.

And in the Land of the Free, no one

Should willingly choose to be poor.

BLACKBERRYING with WILLIE
SUMMER 1855

William Wallace Lincoln was born December 21, 1850 in Springfield and died February 20, 1862 in the White House. He was, by all accounts, the most literate and intellectual of the Lincoln children—the favorite of his father and mother, who grieved deeply over his death. Willie received the same permissive upbringing as the other Lincoln boys, and he was indulged and cherished. Lincoln often took him and the other boys to play in the fields and woodlots behind (due east) of their property at Eighth and Jackson, where the family also kept their milk cow. Mary Ann Todd was rarely called by her full name because it might have been confused with that of her younger sister, Ann Marie. Brought up in an aristocratic milieu, Mary Lincoln did eventually learn most of the household arts, including pie-making, as the president-to-be had an apparent sweet tooth. She was aided in these household tasks by tips from *Godey's*, a popular lady's magazine, and *Miss Leslie's Directions for Cookery*, which could fairly be described as *The Joy of Cooking* of its day.

Mary Ann would have a pie and the vines

Grow faster than childhood, the red fruit

Darkens and sweetens like father-love.

Little Willie is purpled with berry juice,

Our bucket emptied of every fruit.

On the way home, the double-horned moon

Points through the sycamores, it is ours

This marked moment of man and boy,

Whether Mary Ann has her pie—or not.

WINTERING

Mid-nineteenth-century climate was, on the whole, abnormally cold. Even though reliable meteorological statistics do not appear until the 1870's, there is ample anecdotal evidence for the severe winters that appeared in the decades before the Civil War. In Illinois, the winter of 1830-1831 was especially bitter, and it was the first winter experienced by the extended Lincoln family in Illinois. Carl Sandburg has written lyrically about this memorable season in his biography of Lincoln. Old Bob was one of Lincoln's favorite horses. His real name was Robin, and he sported a reddish-brown coat.

Each day the prairie eats more of the sun,

Swallows brightness, buries luminosity

Under the Loam, under darkening seams

Of coal and small crenellated outcroppings.

This is the slow digestion of Life.

Whatever moves, lives, or lightens

The load goes down like that sycamore

Crusted with ice, roaring and cracking

Under its own improbable weight.

Old Bob knows this wisdom, his fine

Ears brushed by falling snow, silver

Hooves marching through the moonlight.

EATING ILLINOIS

Originally, after the founding of the State of Illinois in 1818, the counties were huge and covered hundred and hundreds of square miles. But the residents complained that the county seats were often too far away. Some people had to travel days to obtain a marriage license or have a deed recorded. So the counties split into parts and then split again, like living cells. More and more people moved into Illinois as word of the rich farm land spread eastward—and as technological improvements like the John Deere plow allowed farmers to plow up the dense prairie sod and prairie grass nearly three meters high. Lincoln knew all the Illinois counties that comprised the Eighth Judicial Circuit, and he traversed most of the rest of the state by raft, rail, and horse. He had, in one sense, devoured the state.

The tender parts, the haunch
And liver and sweetbreads,
Are the first to go.
Like counties, their over-cooked
Joints fall apart, meat tattered on the bone,
Smaller and smaller fragments,
Shelby from Crawford, Macon from Shelby
And from Macon itself, Moultrie and Piatt.
The lonely line of separation, the cord
Knotted from mother through sons
To fathers, stretches taut as a tow-line
A clean and legal demarcation
Like townships into counties.
We live as maps,
The menus of the earth.
And under it all the heart beats incessantly
While the river flows in a crooked black line
Even when covered with ice.

THE LOST SPEECH, MAY 29, 1856

Although Lincoln had a reputation in the Illinois legislature and on the Eighth Judicial Circuit for his remarkable oratorical skills, there is no surviving text for the most famous speech he delivered before the Washington years, the so-called "Lost Speech," given in Bloomington on May 29, 1856, at the close of the Illinois State Republican Convention. Lincoln was on fire that evening, speaking with such atypical passion and zeal that he fairly mesmerized his audience. The speech quickly became legendary. Billy Herndon, his law partner, had stationed himself in the audience to take notes, but he threw away his paper and pen, living only "in the inspiration of the hour." Only the *Alton Weekly Courier* published a brief report of the speech, which dealt with the general subjects of slavery and preservation of the union. This major speech stands as one of the few instances when Lincoln spoke extemporaneously. Even his poignant little farewell to the burghers of Springfield on the rainy morning of Feb. 11, 1861, had been planned in advance. Only three months before the delivery of the Lost Speech, Lincoln had met with anti-Nebraska journalists in Decatur, where he directed the writing of the founding documents of the state Republican party. The Lost Speech was fueled by the overpowering feeling that something new was in the air. The event had all the enthusiasm of a religious revival. It was also a telling reminder of the ephemeral nature of language, how the most important statements can be lost in an instant.

Even now, it lingers on the tip

Of my tongue, the words splitting silence

Like an axe blade through hickory.

Suddenly, there is a clearing in the woods,

Light pooling in the cloistered space

And for the briefest moment of grace

We are transcendent and complete

In a godlike communion of Words.

Some truth revealed, we embrace our quotidian

Lives, as the moment fades and disappears.

CHOKE CHERRIES, 1856

The choke cherry (*Prunus virginiana)* is a common tree east of the Mississippi River, usually found growing along fencerows and hedges. It produces brilliant but bitter red fruit, which cooks down into excellent jam and jelly. Lincoln certainly encountered this familiar tree (really a large bush) during his frequent circuit riding and other travels in central Illinois. Choke cherries are abundant along the watercourse of the Kaskaskia River in Shelby County. Lincoln was in Shelby County on August 9, 1856, when he formally debated Anthony Thornton on the issue of slavery. The momentous event was captured in a very large oil painting executed by Shelby County artist Robert M. Root.

The trees are tenanted with red fruit

And October visitors, tourists

From Canada, Michigan, and New York.

Ordinary robins and spattered starlings

Gossiping in strange Northern dialects,

Debating the sectional politics

Of land use and ownership, here

In this grove of choke cherry, fruited

With berries that are acid on the tongue.

They sing of boundaries and the ending

Of the day, an unmistakable note of sadness

That lingers, even in translation.

THE ALMANAC TRIAL

On Saturday August 29, 1857, Duff Armstrong hit James Metzker with a "slung shot" or "cosh" (a hard piece of metal) during an altercation which occurred near the grounds of a religious revival in Mason County. Metzker later died, although the cause of his death was uncertain because he had also been struck on the head by a certain James Norris. Norris was promptly convicted of manslaughter. Duff Armstrong's original attorneys, Dilworth and Campbell of Havana, immediately sought a change of venue in the hope of getting a fair hearing. The trial was then moved west to Beardstown, the county seat of Cass County. Duff's mother, Hannah Armstrong, who had known Lincoln intimately during his New Salem days, engaged her former boarder to defend her son. The trial took place on May 7, 1858, a few months before the famous Lincoln-Douglas debates began. Lincoln deliberately picked young men as jurors because he believed they would be more sympathetic to Duff's cause. Charles Allen was the prosecution's chief witness since he testified under oath that he saw Duff Armstrong commit the crime at eleven o'clock at night while he was standing about 150 feet away. Allen claimed he could see clearly because it was a moonlit night with the moon directly overhead. This position of the moon became a key point in Lincoln's subsequent defense strategy. During his cross-examination of Charles Allen, Lincoln suddenly produced an almanac that indicated the moon had already set at that time on the date of the alleged attack. Furthermore, Lincoln proved that the slung shot in question actually belonged to another man, Nelson Watkins. And, finally, a physician also testified that Metzker's death could have been caused by other factors, such as falling off a horse. Duff Armstrong was acquitted on the basis of this defense, even though Lincoln's reasoning would probably fail today's more stringent forensic standards. It is entirely possible, for example, that the witness *did* see the event clearly, moonlight notwithstanding. Jurors were easier to convince in those simpler times, and the so-called "Almanac Trial" has become Lincoln's most famous performance before the Illinois bar. But the story does not end in Beardstown because a few years later Duff enlisted in the Union Army and then became seriously ill. Hannah Armstrong again appealed to Lincoln, now wearing the hat of the Commander in Chief. President Lincoln discharged Duff Armstrong from service in the Union Army on September 18, 1863, thus saving his life for a second time. This part of the story is taken up by Edgar Lee Masters in "Hannah Armstrong," one of the most memorable monologues in *Spoon River Anthology* (1915). Interestingly enough, Masters was still a practicing lawyer at the time he wrote the poem. In previous centuries, prolonged gazing at the moon was considered to be a cause of insanity or "lunacy." Blackstone's *Commentaries on English Law* was the standard law text of the day, familiar to Lincoln since his New Salem days. Finally, the Almanac Trial is a testament to Lincoln's power of persuasion; his summation completely overpowered the members of the jury.

We are lunatics all, judge and jury,

Prosecution and defense, a little

Moonstruck by all these putative

Facts and figures—now what exactly *is* the Law?

Is Friendship a higher law, surpassing

The statutes of the great State of Illinois?

Does the *Farmer's Almanac of 1857*

Trump Blackstone's *Commentaries*?

Yes, Duff Armstrong may have blood

On his hands, but the ancient Law of Intuition

Pleads eloquently for his freedom, as I look

Into the eyes of the jury and make it so.

NOTES on the AUGUST HEAT

In the summer of 1858, Lincoln and his arch-nemesis, Stephen A. Douglas, began a series of seven debates across the state of Illinois, each man competing for the post of U.S. senator. The sites and dates of their famous debate cycle were as follows: Ottawa (August 21), Freeport (August 27), Jonesboro (September 15), Charleston (September 18), Galesburg (October 7), Quincy (October 13), and Alton (October 15). Although the Government did not record official weather data at that time, local newspapers inform us that for the Ottawa debate the weather consisted of "a breezy, searingly hot day with a scorching sun." This information was ferreted out by Wayne Wendland, who published the results in the Spring 2007 *Journal of the Illinois Historical Society.* Then, as now, Illinois weather fluctuated wildly. Only six days after the Ottawa debate, the two adversaries met in Freeport, where the weather was "damp, chilly, and overcast." The Lincoln-Douglas debates provided an entrée for the relatively unknown Lincoln onto the national scene. Freeport, Galesburg, and Alton were probably his better performances, and Charleston his worst. In Alton, Lincoln concluded by saying that slavery was the real issue, one that would persist "when these poor tongues of Judge Douglas and myself shall be silent." Herb gardens were common sights in the Illinois farm country that Lincoln regularly traversed. The mourning dove (*Zenaida macroura*) ranges through the state.

I.

Gray summer haze

Heavy as a dove,

Lands in the dust of evening,

Then flattens its belly, all the while

Riding gently on the cusp of twilight.

II.

Nose filled with savory, pungent sage,

The sweet scent of marjoram and mint,

And the earthy smells of rust and wood.

III.

It is Hell enough to debate old Douglas

Without the burning flames of August—

This Devil in a clawhammer coat,

Liar and perverter of the English language,

Making a horse-chestnut into a chestnut horse!

Ah, the heat of the moment flares

Into the heat of the day, and we've all

Had our little say in Ottawa, Illinois.

IV.

Screeching cicadas and thrumming katydids,

The unpaid musicians of late August,

Keening and rasping,

Like politicians pleading for election—

Or cursing the bitter aftertaste of Sweet Success.

SOCKS in DANVILLE, SEPTEMBER 21, 1858

In 1855, Dr. William Fithian built a house in Danville, Illinois that later became his office. Like Lincoln, Dr. Fithian was an Illinois legislator in Springfield, and he knew Lincoln quite well. During the Civil War, Dr. Fithian served as a U. S. Army surgeon. In the late summer of 1858, during the hectic season of the Lincoln-Douglas debates, an over-worked Lincoln visited Danville and attempted to give a speech from Dr. Fithian's front porch, but he had earlier suffered from severely swollen feet and could not pull his boots back on, causing him acute embarrassment and momentary panic. Dr. Fithian saved the day by positioning Lincoln on his second-floor balcony in such a way that his socks would not be visible to the crowd below. Although we do not possess the text of that speech, it is probable that Lincoln spoke about the great issue of slavery and its various political and legal manifestations like the Missouri Compromise, the Kansas-Nebraska Act (1854), the controversial Dred Scott case (1857), and "popular sovereignty" (or states' rights) as promulgated by Stephen Douglas, Lincoln's arch-enemy. Danville was the last site in Illinois where Lincoln spoke on his way to Washington, D. C., February 11, 1861.

Feet and ankles swollen like a sycamore tree!

Hot blisters rising up like knots and buds.

Enough talk of Compromise and Constitution!

In this Inferno, no more boundary lines

And demarcations, no more Free and Slave States!

For even a man with swollen ankles and no boots

On his feet knows Evil when he sees it

And can stand up for what is right

Even in his stocking feet, high on a balcony

In Old Danville, Vermilion County, Illinois

AUF DEUTSCH, BITTE!

Any beginning student of German is familiar with the instructor's prodding phrase, *auf Deutsch, bitte* ([say it] in German, please). Abraham Lincoln became interested in the German language in the late 1850's because he considered it to be another gaping hole in his haphazard education—he studied Euclid for the same reason during this time period. Lincoln also had a practical purpose in mind. Because of his close association with German-speaking Gustavus (Gustave) Koerner, the state representative from St. Clair, Illinois, Lincoln came to appreciate the significance and potential of the German immigrant voting bloc, roughly concentrated in the Alton-Jacksonsville-Springfield triangle. This vote was critical to the survival of the new Republican Party since it could offset the Irish vote, which was almost solidly pledged to the Democrats. Lincoln may have also vaguely appreciated the rise of German nationalism in Europe, which grew even stronger in the next decades. Finally, since Mary Todd Lincoln knew French, he may have deliberately wanted to try something different. In any event, he began serious study of the language, and in 1859 he secretly purchased the Springfield German-language newspaper, the *Illinois Staats-Anzeiger* or, roughly translated, "The Illinois State Reporter." That paper was edited by Theodore Canisius. *Realpolitik* literally means "practical politics" although the figurative meaning is "power politics." In *Writing Illinois*, Professor James Hurt makes the observation that the first English settlers had no name for the vast grasslands of Illinois and had to resort to the French *prairie.*

Naturally, there was no word for it—

This soul-swallowing entity of Illinois

Prairie, although *die Steppe* un-

Folds equally well upon the tongue.

Der Himmel well describes the un-

Speakable blueness overhead.

Realpolitik eloquently suggests what

Whigs and Democrats do to one another,

While *Gott* is a solid enough name

For that which I could never understand.

ICE CREAM at the SMITHS

Mary Todd Lincoln's younger sister Ann Marie married Clark M. Smith, a successful Springfield businessman, who owned the C. M. and S. Smith Store on the Old Capitol Square. The Smiths moved into the house at 603 South Fifth Street that was later purchased by Doctor Lindsay, the father of poet Vachel Lindsay. Interestingly enough, the Smith house was built by the same Reverend Charles Dresser who had sold the Lincolns their home at Eighth and Jackson. On Sunday afternoons in the late 1850's, the Lincolns would often walk a few blocks to visit their relatives and socialize while making ice cream. The recipe for strawberry ice cream used here is drawn from Miss Leslie's *Directions for Cookery* (1843), the most popular cookbook of its day (Mary Todd Lincoln owned one). Sugar at this time was not refined like today's white granulated sugar. It was sold in blocks or "loaves." Rock salt, snow, or natural ice were packed into the ice cream churn around a covered vessel called the "freezer." Although the future president did not exhibit much of an appetite for most dishes, Dr. Wayne C. Temple, in *The Taste Is in My Mouth a Little* (2004), argues that Lincoln had a pronounced sweet tooth. These ice-cream socials may have represented some of Lincoln's last peaceful moments before the tumultuous years of the presidency.

Clark, the good merchant, purveys firewood, brown and white

Eggs, oiled leather boots, slouch hats, rock salt and loaves

Of sugar. Mary offers a bowl of pulpy red strawberries

And Clark supplies two pounds of loaf-sugar and half

A gallon of cream so thick it whitewashes the insides

Of his bucket. I add rock salt and chunks of pond-ice.

We talk, filling the churn, grinding-grinding, religion

Weather and politics, grinding-grinding, until the silence

Is purified into ice and sweetness, the cupped coldness

Savored on the tongue, that too-sharp moment, quickly

Melting into impossibility, like the surrounding heat

Rising in vapors over the rain-darkened garden.

SITTING for BRADY, FEBRUARY 27, 1860

In New York City to deliver his Cooper Union Speech, the single most important delivery Lincoln made before his election, the would-be candidate sat for a formal portrait in the studio of Mathew Brady, already the most celebrated photographer in the country, and destined to become even more famous because of his documentary photographs of Civil War battles. Brady's stately likeness of Lincoln, who was then 51 years old, became the model for widely circulated woodcuts, lithographs, and a famous Currier and Ives print. The speech was a thundering success, in spite of Lincoln's squeamishness about his "western" style of pronunciation.

Big one tonight, and it's not what I say

But how I say it, no *fust* for first,

No *cheer* for chair, as in Mister Chairman.

Must sound ed-u-cated (not *eddicated*).

This is New York City, not Kentucky!

But my speech-thoughts are so purified

In my heart that my elongated head and tongue

Must naturally *foller* / follow. My *I-dees*

Will become real Ideas for the Athenaeum.

If words become the clothes of the man,

Then consider my uncomfortable new

Black suit, crumpled into a little suitcase,

More creases than tailored cuttings.

Yet I patiently present myself

At Three Five Nine Broadway,

Studio of Mr. Mathew (one T) Brady,

King of all Daguerreotypists,

Master of the Glass Plate,

Copper Plate and Tin Type,

Professorial man with eyes like a camera,

Glazed and unfocused.

"Look into the lens of the apparatus,"

Says the Image-Maker, as I ponder ugly creases

In my crushed undertaker's suit.

Now who will be lying, Lincoln or the camera?

Oh, allow me to be immortalized as a scare-

Crow man in a tangled black suit,

With wild-boar hair and canine ears.

Well, it's midwinter of eighteen-sixty now

And I'm prepared to launch my Kentucky yawp—

Are they ready for the Genius of the Prairie?

EDWARD A. BARNWELL, PHOTOGRAPHER

On May 9 and 10, 1860, the Illinois State Republican Party gathered in Decatur at a specially built Wigwam on the south side of Central Park, where Lincoln was first nominated for the presidency of the United States. On May 9, Edward A. Barnwell, the local portrait photographer, made a candid likeness of Lincoln, who was then fifty-one years old. The Barnwell portrait is owned today by the Decatur Public Library.

Something's always wrong:

Your face turns into molten wax,

The moles protrude like black buttons,

And your hair resembles a bobtailed mare.

Besides, that slippery silk tie

Meanders over and under a starchy collar

That chokes you like a manacle.

Can't stand still much longer—

Can't bear to look at the after-image,

Positive or negative, a likeness of Lincoln,

Ah, the man who would be President!

Now Barnwell is stiff and pertinacious,

More Undertaker than Photographer.

He pictures you in death-colors, like a corpse,

As if you were already dead, or just about to die.

ASLEEP in DECATUR, MAY 10, 1860

In May of 1856, Lincoln stood on the ground in front of the old log Macon County Courthouse and told Henry C. Whitney, a friend and colleague on the Eighth Judicial Circuit, "Here on this spot, twenty-six years ago, I made my first halt in Illinois; here I stood, and there our wagon stood, with all that we owned in the world." In that summer of 1830, Lincoln made his first political speech, a Whiggish exhortation for improvement of navigation on the Sangamon River. Lincoln was a very young lawyer when he first practiced in the old log courthouse, which was replaced in 1838 by a square brick structure, typical of central Illinois courthouses of the period. The old log courthouse, although much altered and frequently repaired, now stands on the grounds of the Macon County Historical Museum off North Fork Road. In the 1840's and 1850's, Lincoln was a regular visitor to Decatur, often staying with friends or registering at the Revere House (his favorite home-away-from-home), which was originally called the Macon House. Local legend has it that Lincoln liked to buy loaves of bread from his favorite baker in Decatur. In February 1856, Lincoln joined a group of anti-slavery newspaper editors in Decatur and drafted the principles that founded the Republican Party of Illinois. Lincoln was in Decatur again in February 1859 to deliver his lecture on "Discoveries and Inventions," which was also presented in Bloomington, Jacksonville, Springfield, and Pontiac. On May 9 and 10, 1860, the state Republican Party met in Decatur in a hastily constructed "Wigwam" made of canvas and cheap lumber. The convention formally nominated Lincoln for the presidency, although he had slipped off to take a little nap and had to be awakened to accept the honor. Richard Oglesby, a man who became three-time governor of Illinois, was the power behind the scene at this convention, inventing the slogan "Lincoln the Railsplitter Candidate." Lincoln's cousin John Hanks even appeared with rails supposedly split by Lincoln in 1830. One week later, Jesse Fell and Judge David Davis, both of Bloomington, performed similar political functions for Lincoln when he was ultimately nominated at the national Republican convention in Chicago. The City of Decatur became a transportation hub when, in 1854, two railroads finally met up there—the Great Western arriving from Niantic to the west, and the Illinois Central coming from Maroa to the north. During Lincoln's time, Decatur became a bustling manufacturing and agricultural processing center, a role that grew more pronounced in the 1870's, and after World War One, when the cornstarch manufacturer A. E. Staley introduced the Asian soybean to central Illinois and radically altered the landscape. President-elect Lincoln stopped briefly in Decatur on the morning of Feb. 11, 1861, as his train was on its way to Washington.

> Gunsmiths, tinsmiths, blacksmiths,
> And distillers, brewers, toolmakers,
> Coopers and cobblers, newspapermen,
> Methodists, Lutherans, Presbyterians, Catholics,
> English, Irish, and German, crossroads
> Of the Illinois Central and Great Western.

> Under the wigwam lie the rails I supposedly
> Split, the lawyers and farmers I call friends,
> Who would make me the Sixteenth President
> Of the United States, if only I could wake up,
> While the old Sangamon, silent as a watercolor,
> Meanders in this gilded frame we call the Prairie.

BUTLER'S AMBROTYPE, AUGUST 13, 1860

In the summer of 1860, while Lincoln was campaigning for the presidency, Philadelphia artist John Henry Brown was hired to paint an official campaign portrait. He described his visit to Springfield in these words: "We [Brown and Lincoln] walked together from the executive chamber to a daguerrean establishment. I had half a dozen ambrotypes [positive image on a glass plate] taken of him before I could get one to suit me." The ambrotypist and daguerrotypist mentioned here is Springfield's Preston Butler who photographed Lincoln on August 13, 1860. The ambrotype shows Lincoln with atypically neat hair, combed smoothly over his forehead. Campaign badges were made from the photograph and sold for ten cents each or six dollars per thousand.

It's all very personal, you know.

You blink, and the camera blinks back

At you, the rolling eye returns

To haunt you, even the crushed satin

Necktie is honored in timelessness.

For once, they got the hair right.

I'm never this neat in Real Life.

But this isn't real—I'm being

Sold like a piece of soap

Or a view of Niagra Falls.

No matter, for this is America

And I always wanted to become

The first truly modern President.

ON GROWING a BEARD

On October 19, 1860, presidential candidate Lincoln received a letter from an eleven-year-old girl, one Grace Bedell, who lived in Westfield, New York, advising him to grow a beard. He responded in the following way: "As to the whiskers, having never worn any do you not think people would call it a piece of silly affection [*sic*] if I were to begin it now?" Yet he took her advice and grew the beard, which became a trademark not an "affectation," the familiar image on the penny and the five-dollar bill. In February 1861, after his election and while the presidential train was taking a long, circuitous route to Washington, Lincoln stopped briefly in Westfield, called little Grace to come forward, and gave her a big kiss.

Pointed

Like all of my

Public statements,

It is the fur

Of maturity—

The Currency

Of the Nation.

BILLY the BARBER, FEBRUARY 10, 1861

William de Fleurville or William Florville was Lincoln's barber for twenty-four years, his neighbor for a time, and the guardian of the Lincoln home when the family was in Washington. Born in Haiti in 1807, he immigrated to Baltimore in 1820 and learned the barbering trade. In 1831 he arrived in Springfield, setting up shop in 1832. Very successful and visible in the Springfield business community, Billy the Barber was also a flute and violin player, a considerable philanthropist in the growing frontier community, and a composer of serio-comic verses which he published in the *Illinois State Journal*: "Billy will always be found on the spot, / With razor keen and water smoking hot; / He'll clip and dress your hair, and shave with ease / And leave no effort slack his friends to please." His shop was on Adams between Sixth and Seventh. Billy charged fifteen cents to cut the hair of men and boys; twenty cents for girls. He cut Lincoln's hair on February 10, 1861, the day before Lincoln left for Washington. On Dec. 27, 1863, he wrote the President: "Tell taddy [*sic*] that his (and Willy's) dog is alive and kicking. . . ." A *coffle* is a chained gang of prisoners or slaves.

> Billy is mopping my face with a hot towel,
>
> Stropping his straight razor, adjusting the chair,
>
> And I gently slumber as this free black man
>
> Scrapes eight inches of sharp surgical steel

Over the soap-covered vessels of my neck.

Once on the Ohio, I beheld a coffle of slaves.

Three men, two women, and a little girl.

The oldest man had white wooly hair

And his back crawled with gray, wormy

Scars, his eyes filled with the blankness

Of being sold downriver, how many,

How many, are still in coffles?

Billy tries to snip and dress my thatch,

A touch of pomade, a little wet combing,

I feel something like a pressure drop

Before a storm, a squeezed-down moment,

As if everyone suddenly started speaking

A different language or time angrily stopped.

It is the end of slavery. It is today. Is Now.

I tip him two-bits, shake his hand,

Leaving as if nothing has happened

Walking down Seventh Street, utterly

Certain I will never pass this way again.

CUTTING and PASTING

As he did in his political maneuvering, Lincoln was careful and exacting in his writing, taking his time and putting the manuscript through several drafts and revisions. Lincoln also carried notes and ideas, which he called "Randoms," on little slips of paper. He typically inserted these jottings into the lining of his stovepipe hat, a kind of portable desk. During the Washington years, he also stuffed his real desk with countless pieces of paper, including unsent letters. According to Douglas Wilson, author of *Lincoln's Sword*, the President liked to make a preliminary printed copy of a formal address. Then he subsequently scissored the printed speech into blocks of text, between which he inserted his handwritten notes, then pasted the whole sequence onto large sheets of "foolscap" paper. In effect, he "deconstructed" his own text as a way of improving it. Lincoln would probably have been quite handy and comfortable with a modern-day word processor—he certainly understood the logic of revision. Lincoln's "First Inaugural," went through this complex process, with additional commentary from Lincoln's Secretary of State, William Seward, who formulated the phrase "better angels of the nation," famously revised by Lincoln into "better angels of our nature." Lincoln also repeatedly ran afoul of Mr. John D. Defrees, a former newspaper editor who served as Superintendent of Public Printing, the man responsible for printing the final version of the document. Defrees complained that Lincoln's "use of commas was excessive." Lincoln delivered his great speech on March 4, 1861.

The speech is always a work in progress.

Only the dead receive a tombstone text,

Words chiseled into marble. For the living

Write their random notes, tucking them

Into waistcoat pockets, or the lining of a hat,

Even while walking down the avenue.

The hat is metaphor for the mind, comma,

Damn Defrees for tinkering with my text!

Or Seward who is wise but not wise enough

To sense that speech is metaphor for life,

And words arrive as whisperings

From the better angels of our nature.

WILLIE and TAD, SEPTEMBER 1861

Mary and Abraham had four sons: Robert (born August 1, 1843); Eddie (born August 3, 1846), Willie, who was Lincoln's favorite (born December 21, 1850); and Thomas "Tad," short for Tadpole (born April 4, 1853). Only Robert, their firstborn, lived to maturity. Eddie died while they were still residing in Springfield on February 1, 1850, and Willie, who most resembled his father intellectually, died in the White House on February 20, 1862. Mary and Abraham were crushed by the death of Willie. Lincoln shut himself up every Thursday for a year thereafter, just to grieve. Mary sought the help of charlatans and mediums, even holding séances at the White House. Lincoln was a very indulgent—almost permissive father—never correcting or disciplining his sons, perhaps because his own father had been such an abusive taskmaster. Billy Herndon, Lincoln's law partner, complained that the boys ransacked the office and overturned inkwells on important legal documents. He once made the crude observation that Lincoln would even let the boys "shit in his hat." Willie and Tad kept goats, rabbits, and donkeys on the White House lawn. The goats were very fond of the President and would faithfully respond as he called them by name. General George B. McClellan, nicknamed "Little Mac" by his adoring troops, was given to epic bouts of procrastination. Lincoln whimsically remarked that he had a "bad case of the slows." General Irvin McDowell's troops were thoroughly repulsed at the First Battle of Bull Run, July 21, 1861. General McClellan was given command of all the troops in the Washington area six days after the disastrous defeat at Bull Run.

Boyish, they situate a fort on the White House roof,

Playing soldiers in cut-down baggy blue uniforms,

Making war on goats, sheep, and donkeys,

While we are encircled by a rebel phalanx

And real blood pools in creeks and cornfields.

Imaginary battles of childhood vanish quickly

And the small victories are bloodless and free.

Now, if only Little Mac would attack, if only

We'd taken Bull Run that sad pure day in July.

The gentry rode out in gilded carriages, picnic

Baskets filled with champagne and ginger cake.

Then panic, carriages overturned, horses lathered,

Citizens terrified—that's when the Real War began.

FLUB DUBS

By the fall of 1861, Mary Todd Lincoln had already overspent her $20,000 household allowance by $6,800. Doris Kearns Goodwin, in *Team of Rivals: The Political Genius of Abraham Lincoln* (2005), quotes Benjamin French, the Commissioner of Public Buildings, whom Mary had enlisted to speak to the President on her behalf. French reported that the President said " . . . it would stink in the land to have it said that an appropriation of $20,00 for furnishing the house had been overrun by the President when the poor freezing soldiers could not have blankets, and he swore he would never approve the bills for *flub dubs* for that damned house!" Like Jackie Kennedy and Nancy Reagan after her, Mary Lincoln left her mark on the old mansion. When the Lincolns arrived in Washington, the Capitol dome was still under construction. Like the nation, it was a work in progress.

Like a hatless man, the Capitol Dome

Remains uncovered, while canvas-tented soldiers

Sleep on the ice-hard ground, blanket-money

Going to Mary's silver tea trays and sugar bowls,

Heavy candlesticks, gas lamps with glass globes,

Limoges dinner plates, gold-roped tapestries,

Damask curtains, and carpets, carpets, carpets!

Seemingly, there is no end

Of buying goods and making war.

In the slough between the White House

And Potomac, good Washingtonians

Dispose of the odd carcass,

Feline, human, or canine—

How merciful were it mine.

THE BOTTOM is OUT of the TUB

The early months of 1862 marked the nadir of the fledgling Lincoln administration. Everyone was frustrated by the slow and ineffectual maneuvers of Gen. George B. McClellan's Army of the Potomac, which had failed miserably in Virginia. Abolitionists were clamoring for emancipation, and the U. S. Treasury was literally running out of money, stretched to the limit by paying for the salaries and maintenance of 700,000 Union troops. The Treasury was forced to sell off its meager gold reserves to pay the bills, much to the profit of gold speculators in New York. Lincoln called them "sharks." On July 17, 1861, the Government began to print its own paper money, known as U. S. Notes or "Greenbacks." These notes were printed in green ink on one side only, and they were not redeemable for gold specie. The paper notes were formally authorized by Congress on Feb. 25, 1862, in the Legal Tender Act, after Secretary off the Treasury Salmon P. Chase admitted that "the treasury is nearly empty." On Jan. 10, 1862, Lincoln had been speaking to Gen. Montgomery C. Meigs, when he confided: "The people are impatient; Chase has no money and he tells me he can raise no more; the General of the Army [McClellan] has typhoid fever. The bottom is out of the tub."

In Illinois now the Prairie is sculpted

In snow and on bright blue days

The country lanes thaw into black ruts

Scoring the too-white landscape

While Bluestem rattles in the breeze.

But here I am in war-weary old

Washington, a penniless president

Out of luck and out of time. When

Gold and money lose all meaning,

Then what is the meaning of war?

Liken me to the Greenback Dollar,

Printed on one side only—

Invisible on the other.

READING *HAMLET*

One of the main benefits of Lincoln's residence in New Salem was his life-long love of Shakespeare, especially *Hamlet*, resulting from the positive influence of Jack Kelso, who was fond of spontaneously reciting favorite passages. Lincoln also learned to admire *Richard III* and *Macbeth* as well as the poetry of Robert Burns, especially "Tam O'Shanter." During his residence in Washington, Lincoln became quite fond of the theater and liked to discuss stagecraft with actors who visited with him at the White House. According to Francis B. Carpenter, the portrait painter who lived in the White House for six months in 1864, Lincoln expressed sharp criticism of the way many actors slurred over one of the key speeches from *Hamlet*, the soliloquy of King Claudius which begins with the line, "O my offense is rank, it smells to heaven. . . ." That speech was Lincoln's favorite piece in all of Shakespeare. Lincoln may well have responded to the poignant correspondences between his own life and that of the dramatic hero of Shakespeare's famous tragedy, including his unflagging friendship with Joshua Speed and the death of his sweetheart Anne Rutledge. In the midst of the horrible bloodletting of the Civil War, he may well have identified with Claudius, a man who was unable to ask God for forgiveness in spite of his transparent guilt. Someone had to bear the weight of internecine war, and Lincoln may have been confessing his own sense of guilt in his public admiration of this speech. In Shakespeare's day, in the Globe Theatre production of *Hamlet*, the Ghost entered and departed the scene through a trap door in the floor of the stage.

The Ghost comes through the trap door in the floor

And that is your Father, bristling with curses

And commands. There is the faithful Friend

And the doddering old Fool, a common political

Fixture, even here in Washington. Unfortunately,

The woman you love dies young, and the Mother,

Tender and foolish, remarries in a bad match.

There was a war, there is a war, and the King,

Putrescent and culpable, is the prime mover

In a world turned into the simulacrum of Hell.

CONSTIPATION

In his long bio-novel *Lincoln,* Gore Vidal makes frequent allusions to President Lincoln's chronic difficulties with his bowels—and the various preparations he used to assuage his discomfort. While he was still living in Springfield, Lincoln regularly visited Corneau and Diller's Drugstore on Sixth Street, purchasing such nostrums as castor oil, cream of tartar, soda water, ox marrow, liniment, and other products. On December 23, 1860, Lincoln transferred his business to Dr. Melvin's Drug Store at Fifth and Washington, the largest pharmaceutical retailer in central Illinois. Until Lincoln's assassination on April 14, 1865, Melvin regularly sent packages of laxatives to the White House. As Commander in Chief, Lincoln was very much a "hands on" President, locking horns with a series of Union generals, including George McClellan. "Little Mac" was a brilliant manager who created the magnificent Army of the Potomac but—with the exception of Antietam—failed to use it properly, always fearing that Lee outnumbered him in troops and horses. "He has the slows," Lincoln famously uttered. All of these pressures operated on the President most dramatically during McClellan's abortive Peninsula Campaign in southern Virginia in 1862.

How indelicate for the President of the United States

To be hoist upon his privy

While the Army of the Potomac, greatest army

In the world, is stuck in the mud, mired in the pudding

Of Old Virginia.

I have sampled herbal teas, chamomile,

Oil of the castor bean, *cascara sagrada*,

Peppermint and the extract of dried prunes.

Meanwhile, Little Mac will not advance a single inch

Without more wagons, more cannons, more brigades, more horses,

Turning the roads into wheel ruts of yellow mud

All to fight a phantom army of Robert E. Lee!

As always, he has a bad case of the Slows

And I am constipated.

Thus, the War goes on.

JIP

Lincoln loved animals all his life, especially Fido, the family dog in Springfield, and his horses—Tom, Belle, Old Buck, and Old Bob. Lincoln famously rescued a stuck pig rather than endure his pitiful squealing. Lincoln also rescued Tad's ponies when the White House stables caught fire one night. Little Jip, the White house dog, faithfully followed the servant bearing the President's luncheon tray. He then sat up on his hind legs and begged for his expected share of the meal. President Lincoln, to the dismay of his secretaries, was very generous with his time, opening his office door to the general public. He was naturally besieged by office-seekers, journalists, clerics, bureaucrats, congressmen, senators, and military officers. Lincoln did not take any vacation during his presidential tenure in Washington. Like most country folk, Lincoln still called lunch "dinner," and dinner "supper."

Mr. Jip, a trim little fellow

In the canine manner, appreciates

The protocols and manners of daily life.

The White House is a business, after all,

And things must run on Presidential Time.

So, uncomplaining, he sits rigidly

On his haunches, expecting to receive

His dinner and, like his Master, waits

Decorously until he is properly served.

All goes according to Ceremony, even

If Jip sometimes can't distinguish

The servants from the served.

TOM THUMB at the WHITE HOUSE
February 13, 1863

"General" Charles Stratton, thirty-six inches high, was the star attraction of P. T. Barnum's Circus. He married Lavinia Wilson, who stood only thirty-two inches high. To celebrate this marriage—and Valentine's Day—Mary Todd Lincoln invited the diminutive couple to a special party at the White House. According to Daniel Epstein, author of *Lincoln and Whitman: Parallel Lives in Civil War Washington*, most of the Cabinet members attended this gala event, which was well reported by the press. Charles Stratton often depicted the little figure of Cupid, cavorting about the stage and shooting tiny arrows of love at his appreciative audience.

Lavinia is a little beauty in white satin

And massive diamond necklace—Charles

Is attired in simple black with heavy gold watch

And elegant white kid gloves. Two human dolls,

They stand no taller than the bottom

Of my waistcoat—Charles and Lavinia,

Abraham and Mary, twin odd couples

On display in the White House Circus.

Show your ticket and behold two pairs

Of documented freaks, each one shot

By the unerring Arrow of Love, drawn

From the bottomless quiver of Desire.

THE ONE LEGGED MAN
August 11, 1863

On a torrid day in the summer of 1863, President Lincoln encountered a one-legged former slave, who was begging on the dusty streets near the White House. According to Daniel Epstein, Lincoln stopped and wrote a check on the spot for $5.00. That amount would equal over $100 in today's currency. At this time, the city of Washington was swarming with soldiers on leave and refugees from the "slavocracy" of the Confederate South. There was no Federal policy for dealing with this influx of hungry, homeless, and disoriented persons streaming into the nation's capital.

To lose your nation,

Your native tongue, your wife,

Your little children, and everything

Familiar—that is Tragedy enough.

Then to suffer the loss of a leg,

Hobbling around Washington in wartime,

Like a three-legged hound, grateful

For scraps—that is insupportable.

So on Riggs Bank I draw a cheque

For five American Dollars, payable

To the "Bearer," whom I emancipated

Into a life almost as bad as slavery.

PLUG

During the Civil War, soldiers on both sides, of all ranks, tended to discard their official forage caps or dress hats in favor of more personally expressive headgear. General "Jeb" Stuart favored plumed hats with matching sashes. But throughout the nineteenth century, a man's hat was a very important badge of identity. Ward Hill Lamon, the Danville lawyer who later became Lincoln's bodyguard in Washington, observed that the President had "very defective taste" in hats. Lincoln supposedly lost his hat during the inauguration of President Zachary Taylor in 1849. He seemingly had so much trouble with his hat at his own inauguration on March 4, 1861, that Stephen A. Douglas, his opponent and friend, graciously offered to hold it while Lincoln delivered his address. As an everyday frontier lawyer and later as president, Lincoln favored the "plug" or "stovepipe" hat, and employed its capacious interior as a portable file for notes, checks, speeches, drafts of legislation, and personal letters. The office he shared with William Herndon at Fifth and Washington was in a similar state of disarray. Lincoln bought his hats from haberdasher George Hall who operated a shop at Fifth and Adams. The three-day battle at Gettysburg, July 1-3, 1863, literally soaked the earth with blood. Lincoln removed his plug to deliver the Gettysburg Address.

I am the Lincoln Paper Doll; carefully scissor

The farmer's straw hat with its paper tabs,

Folding them neatly behind my head. Follow

The same procedure with the black derby,

The brown slouch, and the navy blue captain's

Cap—no, none of these seems right, so try

The plug, the old stovepipe, portable office

For bills, unmailed letters, undelivered speeches

And addresses, dedications for ordinary ground

Like these wounded hills of Pennsylvania,

Rock, soil, wheat, and water—

All blood-soaked and sacred for eternity.

KECKLY, DRESSING MY HAIR

Elizabeth Keckly, *modiste* or seamstress to Mary Todd Lincoln, was a former Virginia slave who had purchased her freedom and that of her son by dint of hard work and perseverance. She composed a famous autobiography, *Behind the Scenes or Thirty Years a Slave, and Four Years in the White House* (originally published in 1868 by G. W. Carleton and reprinted in 1988 by Oxford University Press). Mrs. Keckly was a remarkable woman who became the most trusted servant of Mary and Abraham. President Lincoln often requested Mrs. Keckly's tonsorial services before events of state. After the President's assassination, she was dispatched to New York to sell off Mary's considerable wardrobe, a futile attempt to raise cash for the beleaguered former first lady. In 2003, historian Jennifer Fleischner published *Mrs. Lincoln and Mrs. Keckly* [sic]: *the Remarkable Story of a Friendship Between a First lady and a Former Slave.*

She flexes her fingers like a concert pianist,

This African queen, teasing grace notes

From my choppy thatch, gracefully playing

Glissandos on my crown. She presses ever so

Close, the joist of her hip touching my ribs,

Her pneumatic bosom swelling

Against my back, her hands fluttering

Over my cheeks and beard. And thus

The Presidential locks lie down in perfect

Harmony as Lizzy strikes the final chord,

Gently withdrawing her hands, stepping

Away, as if to admire her artistry

When, all too suddenly, the music dies.

CARPENTER'S ALLEGORY

Francis Bicknell Carpenter (1830-1900) took up residence at the White House from Feb. 4, 1864 to the end of July 1864. While he was living on the premises, he painted his masterpiece, *The First Reading of the Emancipation Proclamation,* which was originally exhibited on July 22, 1864. The painting now hangs in the U. S. Capitol. Carpenter also executed paintings of the entire Lincoln family, and he wrote a book entitled *Six Months at the White House* (1866). In 1866, Alexander Hay Ritchie made an engraved print version of Carpenter's painting, which sold widely at $5.00 per copy. Carpenter said the painting was a "mingling of fact and allegory," with the Cabinet members arranged so that the "radicals" were on the left and the "conservatives" on the right. Lincoln, of course, is the unifying figure in the center. The painting is littered with symbolic items, including a barely visible portrait of Andrew Jackson at the top center, a map of the war in Virginia at the right side of the table, and copies of Story's *Commentaries on the Constitution* and Whiting's *War Powers of the President* opened and propped against the empty chair on the far right. A copy of Horace Greeley's influential *New York Tribune* is on the floor on the far left. Lincoln is also flanked on the left by Sec. of War Edwin M. Stanton and Sec. Of the Treasury Salmon P. Chase. Sec. of State William H. Seward is placed in the foreground, and Sec. of the Navy Gideon Welles is seated opposite to him. In the right hand corner are gathered Attorney General Edward Bates (at the end of the table), flanked by Postmaster General Montgomery Blair and Sec. of the Interior Caleb B. Smith. The painting was created from a number of pencil sketches and from Mathew Brady photographs. Francis Carpenter made his very first sketch of the whole composition on the back of an old photograph. Abraham Lincoln was a gradualist who embraced emancipation only after it could be justified as a strategic necessity on both military and constitutional grounds. See illustration on page 4.

Time is composed in little dribs and drabs,
The lemony light of linseed, odd patches
Of blue cerulean and zinc white, and the deep
Presidential tones of umber and sienna.

How unlike a photograph, where
The prisoner is shackled momentarily
And then released—while the Painter,
Part sleuth, part jailer,
Stalks the house in burglar fashion,
Lifting bits of conversation, articles
Of clothing, and the very icon of the Soul.

He's shortened my long legs, prettied-up
My tousled hair, softened the war-cracked
Cheeks, retaining Seward's beak of a nose.
The Constitution is standing for Law,
Jackson's portrait for the Presidency,
The war map of Virginia means Rebellion.
The *New York Tribune* is Horace Greeley,
And the *Congressional Globe* for Congress.
These, the seven peevish men who never stood
Silent except in this all-too-fictive world of Art.

OYSTERS at WILLARD'S

Because of the detailed scholarship of John J. Duff, author of *A. Lincoln, Prairie Lawyer,* and Wayne C. Temple, who penned *"The Taste Is In My Mouth a Little . . ."* we are privy to many of the details of Lincoln's workdays and his eating habits. Like most Westerners of his day, he ate a great deal of cornmeal and pork, but he also loved wild game, especially venison—and he had a pronounced sweet-tooth, as shown by his love of lemon custard pie and Mary Todd Lincoln's White Cake, a traditional dessert of the Todd family in Lexington, Kentucky. Lincoln also liked the Todds' famous "beaten biscuits." Since Mary was not broadly educated in the culinary arts, Lincoln bought her a copy of Miss Leslie's *Directions for Cookery* (1843 edition). Lawyer Lincoln first ate oysters (fried) at Chatterton's Restaurant in Springfield. On his way to Washington from Springfield in mid-February, 1861, President-Elect Lincoln stopped at the Astor House in New York City, where he enjoyed stuffed shad and other delicacies. He also stayed at Willard's, the grandest hotel in the city of Washington during the Civil War period. Whenever he had a quiet evening—which was rare in the last years of the Civil War—Lincoln enjoyed chatting with his old friend from Illinois, Orville Hickman Browning, whom he had known since his days in Vandalia as a young politician. Lincoln avoided alcohol all his life, and, according to Billy Herndon (his law partner), he was constantly munching on apples. In the summer of 1864, it was widely believed that Lincoln could not be re-elected, but he won the election handily, running on the Union ticket. Lincoln's Second Inaugural Ball was catered by Mr. G. A. Balzer, who spread table after table with a profusion of gourmet treats and delicacies. The event occurred on the evening of March 6, 1865.

Quail, roasted and stuffed, pyramids
Of Citrons, chocolate Nougats, macaroon
Tarts, ladyfingers, and sweet Claret jelly;
Chicken in black Truffle sauce—tributes
To an improbably elected president.

The Lemon ice is bitter-sweet
Upon the tongue, where it dissolves
Like Memory—ah, Washington,
You corrupter of simple tastes!

Oysters at Willard's were my downfall.
Now of an evening, I crave the honesty
Of plain talk and plainer food—
A wedge of cornbread, some smoked ham,
A green apple and a preternatural glass of Milk.

CITY POINT, 1865

City Point, Virginia was a boat-landing on the James River, south of Richmond and Petersburg. City Point served as the command center and headquarters for General Ulysses S. Grant. Very much a "hands on" Commander in Chief, Lincoln visited Grant at City Point, sailing down the Potomac River, and back up the peninsula on the James. In the early spring of 1865, shortly before Lee's surrender at Appomattox Court House on April 9, 1865, Lincoln visited Grant for the last time, accompanied by Mary and Tad. Lincoln stayed at City Point for two weeks, from March 24, 1865 to April 8, 1865. Lincoln reviewed the troops, visited their encampments, and discussed strategy with Grant. Mary created an unpleasant scene, retreated to her quarters, and pouted. The Union troops cheered Lincoln enthusiastically. These soldiers had cast their absentee ballots in the presidential campaign of 1864, a bloc of votes that helped put Lincoln over the top. "Lorena" was a popular ballad of the day, sung by both Union and Confederate soldiers.

The little white tents spread their wings like moths,

As the gray-blue evening thickens with soldiers

And the sweet smoke of uncountable campfires.

The Old James River tumbles along, smelling

Of turtles and fish, oblivious to the War.

So Victory is a pleasant little boat-ride

Down the peninsula, a lonely trooper singing

"Lorena," and a grossly fat Moon

Falling asleep on the River.

CONTENTS of MY POCKETS, APRIL 14, 1865

Most of these historical data on Lincoln's death can be located on the Library of Congress Website (www.loc.gov) and the National Park Service site on Ford's Theater (www.nps.gov/foth/hwld/htm). Gen. Richard Oglesby arrived in Washington on the afternoon of April 14, 1865, but he was too tired from his train journey to accompany the Lincolns to the performance of *Our American Cousin* at Ford's Theatre. After John Wilkes Booth shot the President, his wounded body was moved directly across the street to the residence of William Petersen. Richard Oglesby (three-time governor of the State of Illinois) was at the bedside throughout the night and was still holding Lincoln's hand when the President died at 7:22 AM on April 15, 1865.

Never was my favorite, Ford's Theatre—

And what little I remember of the comedy

Has collected like mush around that bullet

Lodged theatrically in the whorls of my brain.

Oh, this is not the first time! Please count

The bullet holes in my stovepipe hat . . .

After all, I was an easy target, a too tall

Man on an undersized horse.

And I so wanted to join the Honored Dead:

Every night I walked to the War Department,

Reading the telegrams, the body count—

Balls Bluff, Shiloh, Gettysburg, Antietam.

Future historians, do take note:

I carried a pair of reading spectacles,

Some Confederate *Dix* banknotes

(Where do you think we got *Dixie?*)

And some favorable newspaper clippings—

My vanity required a few nice words occasionally.

And Bill Petersen was ever so kind, how neighborly

Of him to offer that narrow house across the street.

Try to comfort Mother, she grieves so easily.

If only Oglesby had been there, maybe, maybe.

But he's holding my hand now, whispering into my wound

As the windows brighten on a perfect April morning . . .

BULLET in MY BRAIN, APRIL 15, 1865

"Goober Peas" or soft-boiled peanuts were the rations of last resort for the Georgia militiamen during the Civil War. Their song "Goober Peas" became popular on both sides of the Mason-Dixon line, and it was still performed as part of the military repertoire well into the twentieth century:

> Peas, peas, peas, peas,
> Eating Goober peas.
> Goodness, how delicious,
> Eating goober peas!

The bullet from assassin John Wilkes Booth lodged in Lincoln's brain on the evening of April 14, 1865 in Ford's Theatre in Washington. Lincoln died the next morning in the William Petersen House across the street. His body was then brought to the White House where surgeons sawed open his skull and removed the tiny but deadly projectile. It is now believed that Lincoln might have survived that trauma if modern medicine had been available—he may even have recovered and led a relatively normal life. Apparently, the speech center of the brain was not affected. The brain was little understood in Lincoln's day, except for the pseudoscience of Phrenology.

Smaller than a Goober Pea, the leaden

Vessel lies foundering in the Bay of Memory,

Beyond the gravelly shoals of Speech

And the untamed currents of Hysteria.

Identity becomes amorphous, a flattened

Ball of lead spiraling downward,

Downward, until there is no more

Of More—and even History dies.

ALTERNATE ENDING

Funeral services for President Lincoln were held in the White House on April 19, 1865, and the presidential funeral train left the city of Washington on April 21, making its first stop in Baltimore. The rest of the itinerary is as follows: Harrisburg (April 21), Philadelphia (April 22), New York City (April 24), Albany (April 25), Buffalo (April 27), Cleveland (April 28), Columbus (April 29), Indianapolis (April 30), Chicago (May 1), Springfield (May 3). On May 4, 1865, Lincoln's body was placed in a temporary receiving vault in Oak Ridge Cemetery in Springfield. Lincoln's body was buried in a crypt of the still unfinished tomb on September 19, 1871. On October 15, 1874, Richard J. Oglesby helped to dedicate the Lincoln Monument. But on November 7, 1876, three men who had ironically planned their crime in the town of Lincoln, Illinois, attempted to steal Lincoln's body. They were later captured in Chicago and sentenced to a year in the penitentiary. On July 16, 1882, Mary Todd Lincoln died in Springfield and was buried in the Lincoln tomb, where sons Eddie, Willie, and Tad were also buried. On July 26, 1926, Robert Todd Lincoln died and was later buried in Arlington National Cemetery. On the day of Lincoln's first burial in Springfield (May 4, 1865), his favorite horse, Old Bob, marched in the funeral procession, and he was appropriately draped in black. Black crepe and black satin ribbons marked the presidential journey all the way from Washington to Springfield, a somber foil to the bright bunting and the ubiquitous American flags. Before his assassination, Lincoln and Mary regularly attended opera performances presented by New York companies visiting the nation's capital. One of their favorites was Weber's *Der Freischutz*.

No, it wasn't supposed to end this way,

Mourners lining the railroad tracks, miles

Of black crepe and patriotic bunting.

I was supposed to become the Regent

Of Reconstruction, or a Continental tourist

(so I could practice my German on site)—

Even a pilgrim in Jerusalem. Of course,

All the while I'd write my memoirs, making

Obscene profits as a corporation lawyer.

Yet here I am, the Sentinel of Oak Ridge,

Watching the comings and goings, savoring

The passage of Time, which is like snow,

Redesigning the contours of the land, a soft

Tattoo, like prairie showers on cedar shakes

In that other world I once so happily inhabited.

INDEX

A

Albany, New York, 140

Allen, Charles, 84

Almanac Trial, The, 84, 85, 86, 87

Alternate Ending, 140, 141

Alton, Illinois, 88

Alton Weekly, 80

Ambrotype, 102

Andromeda, 64

Angle, Paul, 40

Animals, 29, 30, 31, 35, 40, 41, 56, 57, 66, 67, 71, 76, 77, 106, 110, 111, 118, 119, 120, 121, 136, 140

Antietam, 118, 187

Armstrong, Duff, 84

Armstrong, Hannah, 84

Armstrong, Louis, 58

Army of the Potomac, 118, 119

Asleep in Decatur, 100, 101

Auf Deutsch, Bitte, 92, 93

B

Bachelard, Gaston, 58

Backporch, Eighth and Jackson, 60, 61

Baker, Jean, 52

Baltimore, Maryland, 140

Ball's Bluff, 137

Balzer, G. A., 132

Barnwell, Edward, 98

Bates, Edward, 130

Bauer, Kim, 22

Beardstown, Illinois, 58, 59

Bedell, Grace, 104

Behind the Scenes, 128

Belle (horse), 120

Berry, William E., 24

Bible, The, 36, 73

Billy the Barber, 106, 107

Blackberrying with Willie, 74, 75

Black Hawk War, 20

Blackstone's Commentaries on English Law, 36, 37, 44, 45, 85, 86

Blair, Montgomery, 130

Bloomington, Illinois, 20, 44, 62, 80, 100, 101

Books, 11, 25, 27, 28, 35, 36, 37, 38, 40, 48, 72, 94

Booth, John Wilkes, 136, 138

Brady, Mathew, 96, 130

Branta Canadensis, 66

Brown, John H., 102

Buffalo, New York, 140

Browning, Orville H., 132

Bull Run, 110

Bullet in my Brain, 138, 139

Butler, Preston, 102

Butler's Ambrotype, 102, 103

Burns, Robert, 26, 36, 116

C

"Camptown Races," 68

Canada Goose, 66

Canisius, Theodore, 92

Cartwright, Peter, 60

Carwardine, Richard, 16

Carpenter, Francis Bicknell, 116, 130
Carpenter's Allegory, 130
Cass County (Illinois), 58
Cassiopeia, 64, 65
Cepheus, 64
Charleston, Illinois, 19, 88
Charter Hotel, 34
Chase, Salmon P., 72, 114, 130
Chatterton, Charles, 48
Chatterton, George, 48
Chatterton Jewelry Store, 48
Chatterton's Restaurant, 132
Chicago, Illinois, 58, 101, 140
Choke Cherries, 82, 83
Christian County (Illinois), 50, 51, 59
Christians, Evangelical, 43
City Point, 134, 135
City Point, Virginia., 134, 135
Civil War, 20, 58, 62, 72, 76, 90, 96,
116, 122, 126, 132, 138
Clay, Henry, 52
Cleveland, Ohio, 140
Columbus, Ohio, 140
Commentaries on the Constitution, 130
Constipation, 118, 119
Contents of my Pockets, 136, 137
Corneau and Diller's Drugstore, 118
Crawford Co., 79
Currier and Ives, 96
Cutting and Pasting, 108, 109

D

Danville, Illinois, 44, 80, 90, 91, 126
Davis, David, 44, 45, 56, 101
Daguerre, Louis, 20
Daguerreotype, 20

Decatur, Illinois, 10, 11, 18, 20, 22,
44, 62, 80, 98, 100, 101
Deere, John, 78
Defrees, John, 108
Democratic Party, 24, 72
Deism, 32
Deism in Little Things, 32, 33
Der Freischutz, 140
Descartes, René, 22
Dickson and Sickles, 32
Dilworth and Campbell, 84
Directions for Cookery, 94
Donald, David, 42
Douglas, Stephen A., 24, 52, 70, 88,
90, 126
Dred Scott, 90
Dresser, Charles A., Rev., 48, 52, 94
Duff, John, 132

E

Early American Winters, 19
Eating Illinois, 78, 79
Eaton, 64
**Edward A. Barnwell,
Photographer**, 98, 99
Edwards, Ninian Wirt, 50, 52
Eighth Judicial Circuit Court, 44, 50,
56, 78, 80, 100
Emerson, Ralph W., 32
Epstein, Daniel, 70, 122, 124
Ergo Sum, *22, 23*

F

Farnham, Eliza, 68
Fell, Jesse, 101
First Reading of the Emancipation,

Proclamation, 4, 130
  Fido, 120
  Fithian, William, Dr., 90
  Fleischner, Judtih, 128
  Flub Dubs, 112, 113
  Following in Lincoln's Footsteps, 50
  Food, 18, 19, 21, 37, 44, 46, 47, 59,
73, 74, 79, 83, 89, 94, 95, 100, 111, 132,
133, 134, 135
  Ford's Theatre, 136, 138
  Foster, Stephen, 68
  Francis, Simeon, 48
  Freeport, Illinois, 88
  French, Benjamin, 112

G
Galesburg, Illinois, 88
Gary, Ralph, 50
Geese in Shelby County, 66, 67
Geometry, 64
German language, 92, 141
Gettysburg, Pennsylvania, 7, 8, 126
Gibson, Robert, 28
Globe Tavern, 50
Globe Theatre, 116
Goober peas, 138
"Goober Peas," 138
Goodwin, Doris Kearns, 112
Goose Nest Prairie, 19
Graham, Mentor, 27
Grant, Ulysses, Gen., 134
Great Western R.R., 101
Greene, William, 24
Greeley, Horace, 131
Greenbacks, 114, 115

H
Hallwas, John, 40
Hamlet, 36, 116
Hancock, John, 40
Hanks, John, 18
Harrisburg, Pennsylvania, 140
Harristown Township, 18
Harrell's Store, 18
Harrow, 64
Here I Have Lived, 40
Herndon, Billy, 80
Horner, Henry, Collection, 22
Hummingbirds for Annie, 30, 31
Hurt, James, 58
Hypochondria, 48

I
Ice Cream at the Smiths, 94, 95
Illinois Central R.R., 101
Illinois Historic Preservation Agency,
22
Illinois Staats-Anzeiger, 92
Illinois State Journal, 106
Illinois State Legislature, 24
Indianapolis, Indiana, 140
Inventing Jazz, 58, 59
Irving, Washington, 40

J
Jackson, Andrew, 72
Jacksonville, Illinois, 20, 32, 100
James River, 135
Jane's Piano, 62, 63
Jazz, 58, 59
Jesus Christ, 32
Jip, 120, 121

Johns, Jane, 62
Jonesboro, Illinois, 88
Journal of the Illinois Historical Society, 88

K

Kansas-Nebraska Act, 70
Kaskaskia River, 82
Keckly, Elizabeth, 128, 129
Keckly, Dressing my Hair, 128, 129
Kelso, Jack, 26, 27
Keeping Store With Berry, 24, 25
Kennedy, Jackie, 112
Kirkham's *Grammar, 21,* 30, 36, 37
Know-Nothing Party, The, 72
Koerner, Gustave (Gustavus), 92

L

Lamon, Ward Hill, 126
Last Stop, The, 56, 57
Lee, Robert E., Gen., 119
Legal Tender Act of 1862, 114
Leslie, Miss, 94
Lexington, Kentucky, 50
Life in Prairie Land, 68
Lincoln, Abraham, speeches:
Cooper Union Speech, 96,
Discoveries and Inventions, 20, 100,
First Inaugural Address, 108, Gettysburg
Address, 126, House Divided, 70, Lost
Speech, The, 80
Lincoln, Edward Baker (Eddie), 110
Lincoln, Illinois, 140
Lincoln, Mary Ann (Todd), 74, 112,
132, 134, 140
Lincoln, Prairie Lawyer, 132

Lincoln, Robert Todd, 50, 52, 60, 110
Lincoln, Thomas (Tad), 106, 110
Lincoln, Thomas (Lincoln's father),
18, 19
Lincoln, William Wallace (Willie),
78, 110
Lincoln Monument, 140
Lincoln Pets, (see animals)
Lincoln Square, 18
"Lincoln the Railsplitter Candidate,"
100
Lincoln's Sword, 108
Lincoln-Berry Store, 24
Lincoln-Douglas Debates, 88, 90
Lincoln and Whitman, 122
Lindsay, Vachel, 94
Litany for Mary T., 52, 53, 54, 55
Little Pigeon Creek, 16
Living on the Globe, 18, 19
Long Nine, The, 34, 40
"Lorena," 134
Lost Speech, The, 80, 81
Louisville, Kentucky, 38
Love (in many forms), 21, 31, 48, 49,
53, 75, 116, 117, 122, 123, 132
Love is Eternal, 48, 49
Lovejoy, Elijah, 42, 43
Lovejoy, Owen, 42
Ludlum, David, 19
Lyceum, January 1838, 42, 43

M

Macbeth, 36
Macon County (Illinois), 18, 62, 79,
100
Macon House (Revere House), 62, 100

Mason County (Illinois), 84
Masters, Edgar Lee, 32, 85
McClarey, John, 56
McClellan, George, Gen., 110, 111, 114, 118
McDowell, Gen. Irvin, 110
Meigs, Montgomery, Gen., 114
Melvin's Drugstore, 118
Menard County (Illinois), 59
Mercer County (Illinois), 28
Metamora, Illinois, 44
Methodists, 43
Metzker, Joseph, 84
Milking, 70, 71
Missouri Compromise, 90
Mississippi River, 42, 43
Monticello, Illinois, 44
Moroa, Illinois, 101
Morrill Land Grant College Act, 72
Mount Pulaski, Illinois, 44
Mourning Dove, 89, 90
Mrs. Lincoln and Mrs. Keckly, 128
Mud Hole, 68, 69
Musical Instruments, 58

N

National Park Service, 60
New Boston, Illinois, 28
New Orleans, Louisiana, 58
New Salem, Illinois, 20, 24, 26, 27, 68
New Salem Village, 26, 27
Niantic, Illinois, 101
Norris, James, 84
Notes on the August Heat, 88, 89
New York City, New York, 96
New York Tribune, 130

O

Oak Ridge Cemetery, 140, 141
Offut, Denton, 20
Oglesby, Richard J., 100, 136, 137, 140
Ohio River, 16
On Growing a Beard, 104, 105
Old Bob (horse), 76, 77, 120, 140
Old Buck (horse), 44, 45, 120
Old Buck, 44, 45
"Old Dan Tucker," 62
Old Settlers of Macon County (Illinois), 18
Ottawa, Illinois, 88. 89
Our American Cousin, 136
Oysters at Willard's, 132, 133

P

Panic of 1837, The, 24
Pekin, Illinois, 46
Peninsula Campaign, The, 118
"Perpetuation of Our Political Institutions, The," 42
Perry County (Indiana), 16
Personal Recollections, 62
Peruvian Bark, 18
Petersburg, Illinois, 32
Petersburg, Virginia, 134
Petersen, William, 136, 137, 138
Philadelphia, Pennsylvania, 140
Picturing the Prairie, 20, 21
Piatt County (Illinois), 79
Pigs in Taylorville, 56, 57
Plug, 126, 127
Poems of H., The, 40
Poetics of Space, The, 58

Pontiac, Illinois, 20, 100
Potomac River, 134
"Popular Sovereignty," 90
Presbyterians, 42, 43
Prunus Virginia, 82
Pulling Teeth in Tremont, 46, 47
Purkapile Creek, 32

Q

Quincy, Illinois, 88
Quo warranto, 46, 47

R

"Randoms," 108
Reagan, Nancy, 112
Readings, 36, 37
Reading *Hamlet,* 116, 117
Republican Party, 80, 100
Revere House, 100
Richard III, 36
Richmond, Virginia, 134
Ritchie, Alexander, 130
Rose Record Co., 58
Rutledge, Anne, 30, 116
Rutledge Farm, 32

S

Sandburg, Carl, 76
Sangamo Journal, 48
Sangamon County (Illinois), 40
Sangamon River, 18
Seeds, 16, 17
Seward, William, 108
Shakespeare, 26, 36, 37
Shelby County (Illinois), 66, 79, 82
Shelbyville, Illinois, 44, 66

Shiloh, 137
Simon, John, 30
Sitting for Brady, 96, 97
Six Books of Euclid, 64
Six Months at the White House, 130
Skiffle, 58, 59
Sleeping with Speed, 38, 39
Smith, Caleb, 130
Smith, C. M., 94
Smith Store, 94
Snowbirds, 18
Socks in Danville, 90, 91
Speed, Joshua, 38, 48, 116
Spencer County (Indiana), 16, 36
Springfield, Illinois, 10, 11, 20, 34, 36, 38, 40, 41, 42, 44, 46, 48, 52, 56, 68, 69, 70, 71, 74, 80, 90, 92, 94, 100, 102, 106, 110, 118, 120, 132, 140
Spoon River Anthology, 32, 85
"Sucker State," 40
St. Louis, Missouri 42
Staley, A. E., 101
Stanton, Edwin, 130
Stratton, Charles, 122, 123
Stuart, J. E. B., Gen., 126
Sullivan, Illinois, 44
Surveying, 28, 29
Swett, Leonard, 62

T

Tackett House, 66
Tallman Hotel, 66
Taste Is in My Mouth a Little, The, 94
Taylor, Zachary, 126
Taylorville, Illinois, 44, 56
Team of Rivals, 112

Temple, Wayne C., 94, 132
The Bottom is Out of the Tub, 114, 115
The Intimate World of Abraham Lincoln, 38
Todd, Ann Marie 74
Tom (horse), 120
Tom Thumb at the White House, 122, 123
Treatise on Practical Surveying, 28
Tremont, Illinois, 44, 46, 47
Tripp, C. A., 38

U

Urbana, Illinois, 44

V

Vandalia, Illinois, 34, 35
Vandalia, 34, 35
Vidal, Gore, 118
Vermilion County (Illinois), 91
Volney, Constantin, 32
Volney's Ruins, 32, 36

W

Walsh, John, *30*
War Powers of the President, 130
Washington, D.C., 38, 56, 80, 90, 101, 104, 106, 108, 110, 112, 113, 115, 116, 117, 120, 122, 125, 126, 132, 133, 136, 138, 140
Watkins, Nelson, 84
Weather, 6, 8-9, 18-19, 21, 28, 31, 32, 33, 39, 40, 41, 51, 59, 61, 67, 77, 79, 80, 88, 89, 94, 95, 113, 115, 116, 141, 124
Wendland, Wayne, 88

Welles, Gideon, 130
Westfield, New York., 104
"When the Saints Go Marching In," 58, 59
Whig Party, 24, 57, 72, 73, 93, 100
Whiggery, 72, 73
White, Ron, 70
White House, 140
Whitney, Henry, 100
Willie and Tad, 110, 111
Wills, Garry, 70
Wilson, Douglas, 70, 108
Wilson, Lavinia, 122, 123
Winter of the Deep Snow, 18
Winter of the Deep Snow, 18, 19
Wintering, 76, 77
Wigwam, 98, 100
Writ of Quietus, 56
Writing Illinois, 58, 92

Y

Young Men's Lyceum of Springfield, 42

Z

Zenaida macroura (mourning dove), 88